D1631177

DISCARDED BY
MEMPHIS PUBLIC LIBRARY

MAIN LIBRARY

Memphis and Shelby
County Public Library and
Information Center

For the Residents
of
Memphis and Shelby County

Power Volleyball

for Girls and Women

Second Edition

Janet Thigpen

Newark State College

WM. C. BROWN COMPANY PUBLISHERS
Dubuque, Iowa

PHYSICAL EDUCATION

Consulting Editor

Aileene Lockhart
Texas Woman's University

HEALTH

Consulting Editor

Robert Kaplan
The Ohio State University

PARKS AND RECREATION

Consulting Editor

David Gray
California State University, Long Beach

Copyright © 1967, 1974 by Wm. C. Brown Company Publishers

Library of Congress Catalog Card Number: 73-84328

ISBN 0—697—0717—3

All rights reserved. No part of this publication may be reproduced, stored in a retrieval system, or transmitted, in any form or by any means, electronic, mechanical, photocopying, recording, or otherwise, without the prior written permission of the copyright owner.

Second Printing, 1976

Printed in the United States of America

7856693
MEMPHIS PUBLIC LIBRARY AND INFORMATION CENTER
SHELBY COUNTY LIBRARIES

Art
796.325
T439p

contents

list of figures

preface

Power Volleyball for Girls and Women is a presentation of this fascinating and increasingly popular team sport as it applies to girls and women specifically, but *it also has application for all volleyball players*. Many parts of the book feature the techniques which make power volleyball a challenging and stimulating team game for the talented woman athlete—a team game only recently added to the list of Olympic games and a game whose popularity in the sports world would probably surprise the average American sport enthusiast. Many aspects of the book, however, have particular appeal for the novice player.

Chapter 1, "The Game of Volleyball," is designed to give the student a general idea of the evolution of the game and of the distinguishing features of *power volleyball*. Its status can be ascertained by noting national and international activities and competitions which are conducted by its enthusiastic supporters.

An analysis of the techniques for offense and defense and auxiliary skills utilized on both offense and defense are presented in Chapters 3, 4, and 5. Each technique is described in detail in relation to the *occasions for its use*, the *body mechanics* involved in its execution, *coaching suggestions* for its development, and *drills* to be used in order to improve the performance of the technique. The complicated technique of spiking is analyzed through a series of progressions leading to advanced power spiking. The most commonly used techniques of spiking, set passing, overhand passing, blocking, and serving are further analyzed in relation to *common errors* and *coaching hints*.

Diagrams explain the technique drills and depict strategic formations for various systems of offense, formations for the coverage of vital areas of the court in these situations, formations for receiving the service, and formations for covering strategic court areas in other game situations. Detailed coaching suggestions are given for the various formations.

A special feature of the book, *Modified Games*, Chapter 7, will give the teacher assistance in nurturing the interest and enthusiasm of the unskilled and novice player; opportunities are suggested that enable students to play and have fun while building skill and developing a firm foundation of fundamental abilities.

Warm-up drills are presented and specific activities are designed for this purpose in Chapter 6. *Teaching Progression* (Chapter 8) gives suggestions for a systematic organization and presentation of the skills of power volleyball; these are related to *The Psychology of Coaching* (Chapter 10). The author predicts, in *The Future of Power Volleyball* (Chapter 11), an acceleration of interest in the sport and a continual evolution of techniques. Each chapter contains a summary which will be of value to the student in organizing her knowledge and analyzing her reactions to her reading.

Power Volleyball for Girls and Women was written to give the college student who is preparing to enter teaching or the field of recreation leadership insight into the many facets which comprise the game of power volleyball and a comprehensive picture of the process involved in preparing herself as a leader of a team sport that is fun and challenging for all students, regardless of skill. The book offers ideas about the psychology of coaching, how game situations can be modified, facts about warming up and about conducting a practice session that are relevant not only to volleyball but also to other team and individual sports.

The book offers analyses of advanced techniques and strategies and many suggestions about the psychology of teaching volleyball. These may provide the experienced teacher, coach, or recreational leader with a viewpoint that may differ from her own, and may therefore stimulate creative thinking about areas of difficulty in her own environment.

When the first edition of *Power Volleyball for Girls and Women* was published in 1967 there was no other book on volleyball with *power* in its title. The word describes the current game. With this type of play there has been growing interest in volleyball and rapid evolution of skill and knowledge of players and coaches. This development is most welcome by power volleyball enthusiasts.

The original edition of this book contained a chapter on the differences between USVBA and DGWS rules and suggested implications for strategy and playing techniques because these differences presented a major problem for players, teachers, and coaches. Fortunately, the DGWS rules have been changed over the years and more closely parallel USVBA and international rules, making such a chapter now obsolete.

Some of the terms for playing techniques used in the first edition were coined by the author because there was then no common terminology in existence. The proliferation of power volleyball literature by persons familiar with the techniques, strategies, and terminologies of the rapidly evolving game has now standardized some of these terms. In this second edition there is a concerted effort to use those terms currently in vogue.

Chapter 3 which deals with the spike and offensive formations has been greatly expanded. New progressions, drills, and techniques have been added while those that are now obsolete have been deleted. The major additions deal with the "dink" or "soft spike," a basic offensive formation to aid beginners in conceptualizing systematic team play, and the 5 - 1 and 6 - 0 systems of offense for the advanced player.

Chapter 8, "Teaching Progression," has been vastly expanded to deal more existentially with novice and advanced players. An additional section on working with large numbers of students in a small space is designed to aid those increasing numbers of teachers who face that dilemma.

An entirely new Chapter 2 gives a "thumbnail sketch" of the rules of the game which should aid students in getting an overview of the essential rules quickly. It also includes a brief analysis of players' conceptualizations of the game of volleyball and those processes of thinking which distinguish the power and team player from the "garden variety."

The additional annotated list of figures and illustrations should aid one in locating items of interest with a minimal amount of extraneous searching.

Power Volleyball for Girls and Women is designed basically as a text for those preparing to teach and coach. The contents are organized to facilitate the promotion of insights from that perspective. It can, however, be used by all players who wish to further their knowledge of techniques, formations, and strategies.

KEY TO DIAGRAMS

⚲ ············· Player (usually a set passer)

● ············· Player (usually a spiker; sometimes teacher or leader); arrow indicates direction player is facing

○→——→ ············· Movement of the player

– – – – → ············· Movement of the ball

⚬→——→⑥→ ············· Movement of a player from her original position (dotted circle) to a modified position

LF ············· Left forward player

CF ············· Center forward player

RF ············· Right forward player

LB ············· Left back player

CB ············· Center back player

RB ············· Right back player

chapter 1

The Game of Volleyball

Volleyball was originated in 1895 at the YMCA in Holyoke, Massachusetts. The director, William G. Morgan, wanted to give businessmen an opportunity to exercise indoors with a game less strenuous than the popular game of basketball which had been invented in 1891 in nearby Springfield, Massachusetts. His invention utilized a tennis net, elevated to a height of six feet six inches, and the rubber bladder of a basketball which was batted across the net. This brief description of the game would not stimulate one's desire to observe a volleyball game nor would it particularly challenge a good athlete.

Since its inception, however, volleyball has undergone amazing changes. From its small beginning it has now developed into a challenging team game of Olympic stature. A view of the teams participating in the annual national tournament sponsored by the United States Volleyball Association would leave the spectator thrilled with the spectacle of volleyball. The development from the original game of "batting the ball across the net" to the present fast, exciting, invigorating team game with highly specialized individual skills is interesting to the spectator and challenging to the well-skilled performer. Unfortunately, one still has no difficulty in watching the game played as it was originally conceived; yet, with a little effort an entirely different game can be seen—a game that will leave the sport enthusiast with an exciting new sport experience and new skills to master.

POWER VOLLEYBALL

Just what is power volleyball? It is, first of all, a team game in the truest sense of the word. It involves twelve individually skilled players (six on each of two teams) with specific responsibilities, maneuvering in definite, planned and strategic offensive and defensive patterns. Each offensive play depends upon a good pass from the service or spike receiver, a good set pass, and a well-timed and executed spike. The failure of any one of these plays affects the other and gives the opposing team the opportunity to take the offensive with little difficulty. The spiker is the spectacular hitter. She receives the applause and major attention of the spectators but also is the first to understand that she is powerless without the support and skill of her teammates. A weak player on a volleyball team is immediately apparent—it is much easier to camouflage a weak basketball player. In the latter case the team can "play around" her, but this is not true in volleyball. The opposition quickly discovers the weakness and serves and spikes to that weakness.

When playing power volleyball, just getting the ball over the net is not enough. The opposing team takes the offensive with devastating results. The team on defense against a power team has one mark against it to begin with, because it is difficult to receive a well-spiked ball with sufficient control to give the set passer an adequate pass.

Power volleyball is composed of definite, planned and strategic offensive and defensive patterns. Each player has a designated assignment in terms of spiking and set passing. Each court position carries with it a specific offensive and defensive responsibility. The effectively-coached team member understands these specific patterns and responsibilities. She knows where she is to be in any given situation. Her movements are purposeful and she moves constantly while the ball is in play. In short, *power volleyball* is volleyball played with more precision, more strategy, more advanced techniques, more color and skill—more "power"—than is observed in most volleyball games. The "power" comes specifically from spiking the ball. Highly skilled players, both men and women, spike so that the volleyball travels at amazingly high rates of speed—often at rates approaching sixty-five miles per hour!

A criticism of volleyball has been that it is a slow moving game requiring little action. This is the fault of the players and/or teacher rather than a part of the framework of the game. Volleyball has not attained the same kind of popularity enjoyed by other team sports such as basketball, baseball, and football in the United States. Perhaps this is because not many have yet acquired an appreciation for, and knowledge and skills in, the more advanced techniques of power volleyball.

THE INTERNATIONAL SCENE

The ancient Greeks promoted the basic instinct of play and glorified it in the Olympic Games. Some of today's sports began at that time, some even earlier. Volleyball is a young sport in comparison with many others. It seems rather ironic that volleyball, a game originated in the United States, enjoys more popularity in many other areas of the world than it does here. The International Olympic Committee authorized volleyball as an official Olympic sport in 1957. Since the tendency then was to eliminate rather than add activities, the inclusion of volleyball indicates its popularity in the sports world at large. Study of the results of tournaments (pages 131–141) plainly shows that volleyball is not only more popular in other parts of the world but also that the most skilled teams are not from the United States.

Most of the highlights of volleyball on the international scene have occurred in recent years. The International Volleyball Federation was formed in Paris in 1947. The first world volleyball championships were organized for men and were held in Prague, Czechoslovakia, in 1949. The first world championships open to women were held in 1952 in Moscow. In 1955 volleyball was included in the Pan American Games at Mexico City. Games for both men and women were a part of the 1964 Olympic Games in Tokyo, Japan, the 1968 Games in Mexico City, and the 1972 Games in Munich, Germany.

THE NATIONAL SCENE

The United States Volleyball Association (USVBA) does more than any other single organization in this country to promote high-level participation in volleyball. Since 1928 USVBA has sponsored the national championships each year. The first tournament was held in Brooklyn; since then it has been conducted each year in a different locality. Cities bid for the national championships much as they do for the Democratic and Republican political conventions. The championships continue for four days typically starting at 8:00 a.m. and ending at 11:00 or 12:00 p.m., with games in progress on four or five courts simultaneously. The national championships are actually six double elimination tournaments conducted concurrently:

1. The YMCA Championships for members of that organization
2. The YMCA Masters' Championships for members over thirty-five years of age
3. The Armed Forces Championships for men in all branches of the military service
4. The Men's Collegiate Championships for men's teams from any college or university
5. The United States Open Championships for teams from the four previously mentioned men's championships
6. The Women's Championships for women, inaugurated in 1949 at Los Angeles and open to all women

At the time of the national championships the USVBA Committee on Recognitions and Selections commends outstanding players by selecting the *All Americans*. The All Americans consist of:

1. First team, second team, and the honorable mention team from the YMCA and women's divisions
2. First team and honorable mention team from the Armed Forces, YMCA, Masters', and Collegiate divisions

Certain areas of the country consistently have produced the national champions—primarily Chicago, Hollywood, Houston, Los Angeles, and Stockton. For many enthusiasts volleyball is the form of recreation; these payers seem to congregate and perpetuate good volleyball.

Power volleyball gained popularity during World War II. Directors of physical training programs found that it was a very popular sport and promoted it. Clinics and tournaments produced some excellent players. Some of the most exciting and thrilling games in the national championships are in the Armed Services division.

Volleyball as a varsity sport is still by no means as widespread as basketball but it appears on additional college campuses each year. Though the United States still does not compete favorably with Russia, Japan, and other foreign competitors, the enthusiasm generated by the players, coaches, officials, and officers of the USVBA is increasingly evident. More teams enter the national championships. The improvement in skill from year to year is noticeable. More colleges field varsity teams. The caliber of play of college and university women is improving. All these factors point to a brighter future for volleyball in the United States.

VALUES OF VOLLEYBALL

Because volleyball is a game which requires little and inexpensive equipment it is one of the most practical of all sports; it fits into the budget of all schools, colleges, YMCA's, recreational departments, and playgrounds. Furthermore, unlike most sports, the game can be played outside as well as in the gymnasium. In California the game of doubles is also popular, and both games are played extensively on the beaches where the player can get a tan while engaging in stimulating physical activity. More volleyball enthusiasts are found there than in any other state.

In recent years it has become evident that the fitness level of the American people should be improved. President Eisenhower and President Kennedy did much to encourage attention to this problem. Presidents Johnson and Nixon followed their lead. Physical educators have made a concerted effort to improve their programs and to encourage students to acquire skills which can be utilized after school years when opportunities for sports are limited. Since the equipment for volleyball is relatively simple, it is easily accessible. The game can be played by youngsters, appeals to adults of all ages, and is excellent as an activity for coeducational play. Basketball, which appeals to a great number of school-age Americans and to the young adult, is rarely played past age 25 because the strenuous running requires a peak of fitness that is difficult to maintain. Volleyball, however, can provide ample opportunity for rest together with enough activity to promote physical fitness. Anyone observing the national tournament would be impressed with the number of men and women past 35 who play a very skillful game in which experience contributes to effective teamwork and morale.

In most areas of the country the skilled high school age young lady participates in basketball because the general public is conditioned to basketball. Physical educators have done a good job in promoting that sport, and the majority of the schools have at least one coach who feels confident in his or her ability to coach it. This same skilled athlete probably plays volleyball in a class situation, in intramurals, and perhaps in a recreational setting but is not challenged by the typical game. Once she experiences the thrill and excitement of this game with other skilled athletes who have gained proficiency in individual techniques, have a concept of court position in offensive and defensive patterns, and express enthusiasm for vigorous competition in a team situation, however, she becomes a convert.

Professional women physical educators frequently lament the fact that much of the coaching and officiating of sports for girls has been assumed by men, and believe that for psychological and physiological reasons girls' athletics should be conducted by women. In many cases the men do not actually seek this additional responsibility. A community pressures the school administration to provide athletic competition for girls and often the woman physical educator does not feel competent to compete with male coaches. In basketball in particular, few qualified women officials voluntarily expose themselves to a situation where public sentiment is at a very excitable level and male coaches predominate.

In volleyball, however, the men have not yet assumed a dominant role in coaching and officiating and spectators are not so enthusiastic and threatening. The majority of women physical educators are relatively qualified and willing to assume this responsibility. This is an excellent time for women to get in "on the ground floor" to promote a game for girls and women which contributes so extensively to human growth, development, and wholesome use of leisure time. There is unlimited opportunity for the enthusiastic young woman coach to develop the skill of players so that they can have a lifetime of enjoyment and participation in a sport adaptable to family situations as well as to national and international competition. A great deal of pioneering is needed in promoting a framework that encourages competition at the district, state, and national level so that the United States can compete favorably with other nations of the sports world.

NATIONAL ORGANIZATIONS

The United States Volleyball Association (USVBA) is an organization of men and women dedicated to the promotion of a sport they consider worth their untiring efforts—a dedication they accept and assume with only the thought of sharing its enjoyment and benefits with fellow Americans and sports lovers the world over.

Its executive committee is composed of approximately 15 men and women plus representatives from 15 affiliated organizations interested in sports promotion. The latter include the American Association for Health, Physical Education, and Recreation; the National Amateur Athletic Union; the National Athletics; the National Collegiate Athletic Association; and the National Recreation Association. The Board of Directors of the USVBA includes official representatives from these organizations.

A glance at the names of the standing committees will give the individual unfamiliar with the organization an idea of the scope of the work. These include Budget and Finance; Women's, Girls', and Co-ed Volleyball; Equipment and Supplies; International Relations and Selections; Rules and Interpretation; Constitution and By-laws; Player and Team Eligibility; and USVBA Representatives to Other Organizations. Approximately 150 men and women serve on these committees.

The most obvious results of these committees include:

1. Publication of the annual *USVBA OFFICIAL GUIDE* which can be obtained from USVBA Printer: Box 109, Berne, Indiana, 46711. It contains the official rules, articles, and an explanation of the membership and purposes of the organization
2. Sponsorship of annual regional and national volleyball championships
3. Promotion of American participation in international competition
4. Dissemination of information through clinics, publicity, visual aids; accessibility of personnel capable of aiding those who request assistance, etc.
5. Recognition of individuals who make outstanding contribution to the sport

Another national organization instrumental in the promotion of volleyball is the Division for Girls and Women's Sports (DGWS), a division of the American Association for Health, Physical Education, and Recreation. Its purpose is to aid administrators, teachers, leaders, and participants in all girls' and women's sports, not volleyball exclusively. Its Executive Council is composed of four officers and approximately thirty district and area chairmen. Literally thousands of women work voluntarily for this organization.

For the sport of volleyball there are approximately 12 committee members who collaborate with a chairman from each state to accomplish the objectives of DGWS relative to this sport. Some of the more obvious contributions of DGWS committees are:

1. Publication of the *Volleyball Guide* each two years. It includes rules, modified rules for less skilled or young players, articles, a list of organizational committees and officials, and officiating techniques. This guide can be obtained from AAHPER, 1201 Sixteenth Street, N.W., Washington, D.C.
2. Formulation and dissemination of principles and standards of conduct to guide administrators, leaders, officials, and players

Since 1970 the Association for Intercollegiate Athletics for Women (AIAW) and the DGWS have sponsored an annual national tournament for college women which has made a significant impact.

The original edition of this book contained a chapter contrasting USVBA and DGWS rules with pertinent implications for strategy and playing techniques. This was important because many women physical education majors who were future physical educators and recreation leaders participated in class, intramural, and extramural volleyball governed by DGWS rules and then entered schools or recreation centers where they worked with teams using USVBA rules. Before 1957, the rules were different enough to require a relatively long period of rule study and strategy reorientation for the effective transition from one set of rules to the other. In 1957, the former official DGWS rules became known as the *modified rules* and were suggested for young and less skilled players. Additional rule changes in the 1963–1965 *DGWS Volleyball Guide* brought the two sets of rules even closer together. The rule changes in the 1969–1971 *DGWS Volleyball Guide* left only a few differences which are of relatively little importance. The current edition of *Power Volleyball for Girls and Women* does not contain a chapter pertaining to rules and strategy difference. In the opinion of the author, the elimination of the necessity of such a chapter is decidedly an advantage for the advancement of the game. The fact that all players are playing the same or very similar game will aid immensely in promoting the growth of skill in volleyball players and in promoting the game of volleyball.

SUMMARY

1. Volleyball was originated by William G. Morgan in 1895; from its beginning of batting a rubber basketball bladder across a net it has developed into a challenging team game.
2. Power volleyball involves 12 individually skilled players with specific responsibilities, maneuvering in definite, planned, and strategic offensive and defensive patterns.
3. The relatively young game of volleyball has gained Olympic status and the most skilled world competitors are the Russians and the Japanese.
4. The most important single national event is the USVBA National Championships, held in a different city each year.
5. Volleyball is valuable because:
   a. The game is adaptable in terms of facilities and equipment.
   b. The game appeals to males and females of all ages and can aid in the development and maintenance of physical fitness.
   c. Power volleyball is a game which challenges the superior female athlete.
   d. The majority of women physical educators are more willing to assume the coaching and officiating roles for volleyball than for basketball.
6. The USVBA and the DGWS are the two major organizations promoting volleyball and disseminating information useful to players, teachers, coaches, officials, and administrators.

chapter 2

Overview of the Game and the Rules

The official tosses a coin for the captains of the opposing teams; the captain who calls the coin correctly chooses (1) whether her team is to serve first in the first game *or* (2) which side of the net her team is to occupy for the first game. The other captain has the choice not made; that is, if the captain winning the toss chooses to serve, the second captain can choose her court.

The game begins when the referee announces that play is to begin and this is accomplished by a serve by the right back player from *behind* the end line of the court. The timer starts the game clock when contact is made with the ball on the serve and stops it when the ball is dead (temporarily out of play)—which is indicated by the referee's whistle or the ball's hitting the floor. When the original serving team loses its serve, the opposing team commences to serve and continues to serve until it, too, loses its serve by committing an error or a violation of the rules. The timer continues the process of starting the game clock with the serve and stopping it on a dead ball. The players of the original serving team then rotate in a clockwise direction; the server is then the original right forward; the original right back becomes center back, etc. Upon the loss of this team's serve, the original receiving team rotates and begins its term of service. This process continues until the *game* ends: *either* one team has fifteen (15) points with a two (2) point advantage *or* playing time (eight minutes) has elapsed and one team has a two point advantage. If playing time elapses and neither team has a two point advantage, play continues until one team *does* have a two point advantage, regardless of the amount of time involved.

After the first game is completed, the teams exchange sides of the net and begin play in the second game of the *match* upon the referee's signal. The team which did not serve first in the first game does so in the second. At the end of the second game, the winner of the match may or may not have been determined. One team must win the *first two (2) games* or *two (2) out of three games* to be declared the winner of the match. Should the third game be necessary, the teams exchange sides of the net and the team which served first in the first game will begin the service. The teams will exchange sides of the net when half the game has been completed—eight (8) points for one team or four (4) minutes of playing time have expired (if the ball is in play at the expiration of four minutes, the timer will sound her horn on the next dead ball thereafter).

Only the *serving team* can *score*. For example: (1) team A serves the ball; team B commits an error or a violation of the rules; team A scores one point. (2) Team A serves the ball; team A commits an error or a violation of the rules; team B wins the serve (side out). Team B *does not* win a point. This can be accomplished *only* if Team B serves the ball and team A commits an error or violation of the rules. If both teams commit an error or violation simultaneously, the referee orders a replay and neither team is awarded a point; the *same player* who served the ball *prior* to the double error or violation re-serves the ball.

As has been stated, the referee declares the ball dead (temporarily out of play) when an error (foul) or violation of the rules occur. Some of these major errors and violations follow. This is not a completely definitive list; annual rule changes (both in USVBA and DGWS rule guides) make minor adjustments in the rules. The coach or teacher should keep well informed of these changes and pass them on to players, changing game strategies where necessary.

FOULS AND VIOLATIONS

Out-of-Position

1. Server is out of the service area when she contacts the ball.
2. Players of the serving team purposely block (screen) the view of the receiving team on the service.
3. Player is out of rotation order on the court when the ball is contacted by the server.
4. A back court player (LB, CB, or RB) *spikes* from the forecourt (leaves the floor from in front of the back court spiking line which is ten (10) feet from the net) or attempts to *block* at the net.
5. Player serves out of turn.
6. Substitute player re-enters the *game* in a position other than her original place in the serving order.

Serving

1. Player does not hit the ball clearly or legally with the arm.
2. Serving the ball so that it goes out of bounds, into the net, outside of the net, or under the net.
3. Delaying the game unnecessarily.

Net Play

1. Player contacts the net or its supports while the ball is in play.
2. Player reaches over the net to contact the ball before the opponent completes her attack.
3. Player touches the floor on the opponents' side of the net (*beyond* the center line).
4. Player touches the ball or opponent *under* the net to interfere with her play.

Fouls or Violations on Other Plays

1. Hitting the ball illegally (not hitting it clearly)—a push, carry, lift, throw.
2. Hitting the ball out of bounds.
3. Hitting the ball twice in succession (except when players simultaneously hit the ball).
4. Playing the ball in excess of three (3) times before it crosses the net.
5. Allowing the ball to touch the floor *inside* the court.
6. Hitting the ball across the net *outside* the side line markers.
7. Causing the ball to hit the ceiling or overhead obstructions.
8. Hitting the ball with any part of the body below the waist.

Time-out and Substitution Violations

1. Taking more time-outs than allotted.
2. Entering the game too many times.
3. Substitute does not report to the scorer.

Conduct of Players, Substitutes and Coaches

1. Purposeful distraction of an opponent trying to play the ball.
2. Derogatory remarks or acts.
3. Team representative (other than the six players) enters the court while the ball is in play.
4. Attempts to delay the game.

CONCEPTUALIZATION OF THE GAME

"Volleyball" as played in most situations is not a game that appeals to good athletes. It is in large measure played as an individual game with six individuals grouped together against six other individuals grouped together. Occasionally one of the group of six individuals will help another of her group to get the ball over the net if the first player doesn't. Players spend most of their time standing around watching the ball being played by someone else (usually thrown), watching it hit the floor and then lunging as though trying to catch it as it rebounds from the floor, rotating into a different position, and taking one's turn to serve. Often there is some degree of excitement—particularly if there are two or three girls on each team who can get the ball across the net a couple of times after a serve and can motivate a little stimulation thereby—but most of the players are uncertain of what they are supposed to be doing and why. If one or two of the girls in a group of six attempt to get any kind of "team work" going, they become so discouraged that they immediately revert to individual play. One gets the impression from observing that the players think that the ball is "hot" and needs to be gotten out of one's court as soon as possible. The thought process seems to be "over the net," "over the net!"

In contrast to this, "power volleyball" players with some degree of individual skill in playing the ball think "pass the ball," "set it up," "spike it," "block it!" The entire concept of the game is different. "Pass the ball" and "set it up" implies that one has a specific job—in relation to someone else. "Spike it" necessitates the cooperation of teammates to get the ball into spiking position. These players learn to cooperate— not to fight each other for the opportunity to "get it over the net" (should they be so aggressive). This type of game is challenging to the athlete or girl with good physical coordination because (1) there are definite skills to be learned or refined, (2) one learns where she should be in the court for various types of situations, (3) she can depend upon her teammates to cooperate most of the time, (4) she gets satisfaction from contributing to a well executed team play, and (5) IT'S FUN!

3

Offensive Techniques

TECHNIQUE ANALYSIS AND DRILLS

The Spike

A spike occurs when the ball is hit downward with force into the opponents' court. When executed with skill and force, this technique is one of the obvious distinctions between "power volleyball" and volleyball. The spike is the "kill" play of the game and is largely responsible for the winning of points.

This technique is difficult to master because of the fine sense of timing it requires. The spiker must maneuver her body into a desirable position in relationship to a moving ball, jump as high as possible, and hit a moving object while her body is in motion. In addition, she must judge and direct her spike in order to evade blockers on the opposing team or to "play the block" to her advantage (see the photographs of the game between the United States and Rumania on page 67 and of the game between Japan and the USSR page 77).

Even a good athlete will have difficulty in developing the timing and potential power of the spike. *Patience, perseverance, good progressions, and continuous practice are essential.*

Teaching Progression

1. Arm and hand movement
2. Body rotation
3. Spiking against the wall
4. "Spike type" hitting from mid-court
5. Coordination of approach, arm and hand movement, and the rotation of the body
6. Spike across the net
7. Spike a set pass
8. Advanced power spiking

Arm and Hand Movement

Body Mechanics

1. Open the hand, move it to a position behind the head with the elbow lifted to about shoulder height. The wrist is "cocked" so that the back of the hand forms an approximate 90-degree angle with the lower arm.
2. Begin to straighten the arm at the elbow and move it forward.
3. The biceps should travel forward close to the ear.
4. Contact the ball.
   a. The hand is directly in line with the shoulder joint (that is, it is *not* directly above the head and is *not* farther from the head than the shoulder joint to the side).
   b. The hand is in front of the body (closer to the net than the remainder of the body), with the wrist still "cocked."
   c. The elbow is fully extended.
   d. The *heel of the open hand* contacts the ball at 1:30 or 2:00 on the imaginary clock face.
   e. The wrist is snapped forward so that the extended fingers close over the ball to direct its flight downward and to impart top spin.
5. The arm and hand follow through forward and downward a short distance.

Coaching Suggestions

1. Convince the spiker that she can hit the ball just as hard with the heel of the open hand as with the fist.
2. Hitting with the heel of the open hand then the extended fingers allows the spiker to direct the spike with the extended fingers and gain a great deal of control. These two contacts (heel of hand then extended fingers, accomplished by a forward snap of the wrist) are so rapid and close together that they appear to be one movement as one observes a skillful spiker.
3. The position of the hand in the backswing is the same as for a tennis service.
4. The snapping of the wrist forward immediately after the initial contact with the heel of the hand also imparts top spin which is instrumental in bringing the ball downward on a hard driven spike so that it does not go beyond the end line.
5. Maximum leverage and power are obtained only when the hand in contact with the ball is directly in line with the shoulder and in front of the body.
6. The position of the heel of the hand on the ball at contact determines

its flight direction—a 3:00 position and power will send it over the end line.

7. The follow-through is necessary to ensure power to the spike.

8. The analogy of a clock face can also be used to illustrate the position of the arm in relation to the body when contact with the ball is made and for the follow-through. As the arm moves forward from its backswing position, the full extension of the arm directly over the shoulder joint represents 12:00; a position in which the extended arm has moved forward and is parallel to the floor represents 3:00. When the heel of the open hand contacts the ball for the spike it is at approximately 1:30. The follow-through takes the arm to about 3:00. (See the photograph of the game between the United States and Korea, page 51.)

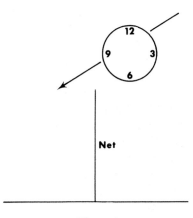

Figure 1

9. If the ball is contacted at 12:00 in the arm swing there will be a *drastic reduction of power* and an illegal hit (a throw) is likely to occur.

Illustration

Figure 1 compares the ball to a clock face to illustrate the desired contact point.

Figure 2 illustrates the analogy of a clock face to demonstrate arm position as it moves forward from its backswing position behind the head.

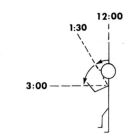

Figure 2

Body Rotation

Body Mechanics

1. The body is facing the net at an approximate 45-degree angle as the hand and arm move backward into position.

2. As the arm begins to straighten and move forward the body rotates at the shoulders and hips so that they will face the net.
3. On impact and follow-through the body faces the net squarely.

Coaching Suggestions

1. The rotation allows maximum leverage and power.
2. To determine an approximate 45-degree angle, turn the left side to the net and then turn the feet to the left about halfway between that initial position and a position squarely facing the net.

Drill

Students line up facing a wall or net with the instructor or demonstrator in front. The arm and hand movement with body rotation is practiced without a ball.

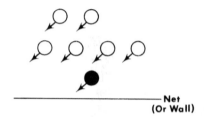

Figure 3

Spiking Against the Wall

Body Mechanics

1. The spiker faces the wall at a 45-degree angle.
2. Simultaneously toss the ball upward with the left hand and begin the arm and hand movement with body rotation.
3. Contact the ball so that it hits the floor and rebounds from the wall.

Coaching Suggestions

1. The purpose of this drill is to give the spiker the experience of proper arm, hand, and body movement *without* the added difficulty of moving to an advantageous spiking position in relation to the ball and jumping.
2. The instructor should encourage the spiker to *toss the ball to the height at which she will contact it* and to *toss the ball well in front of the mid-line of the body* so that she will be able to hit forcefully.
3. If the ball is directly above the body, the player will be unable to get any power on the spike.
4. Spike the ball so that it hits the floor approximately five feet from the wall and rebounds from the wall to the spiker.
5. As the spiker develops skill, she should be encouraged to attempt to spike the ball after it has rebounded from the wall and keep it moving as long as possible between tosses.
6. The instructor should emphasize that height of the ball at contact is

not the important factor as long as the ball is at least shoulder high when it is hit. At this stage the spiker needs to experience power on the hit.

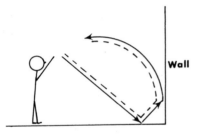

Figure 4

Drill

Figure 4 illustrates spiking against the wall.

"Spike Type" Hitting from Mid-Court

Drill

Players are placed in a formation similar to that described in Figure 7 (p. 23) *except that #1 is back about mid-court* (15 feet from the net) and the "tosser" is *slightly* in front of her.

Body Mechanics

1. The spiker is at an approximate 45-degree angle to the net.
2. The "tosser" tosses the ball so that it makes a high arc about six to eight feet higher than the spiker's head and descends so that it is *slightly in front of and in line with the spiker's* shoulder joint.
3. The spiker executes the proper arm and hand movement with rotation of the body to send the ball over the net.
4. The contact point for the heel of the hand on the imaginary clock face of the ball is approximately 4:00. This differs from the contact point for wall spiking *because the ball is being hit forward and not downward.*

Coaching Suggestions

1. This drill is designed to give the spiker an opportunity to experience a coordination of the backswing, extension of the elbow as the arm swings forward, and contact with the heel of the hand followed immediately by a wrist snap and contact with the extended fingers to impart over spin without the additional difficulties inherent in running forward and jumping.
2. As proficiency in the necessary coordinations is gained, additional force can be applied.
3. The spiker should not jump but should *remain on the floor.*
4. This is the same type of hit as described in chapter five as "one hand overhead for distance." Even short players can use it and the technique has uses other than as a lead-up to jumping to spike downward.

5. The forward snap of the wrist to allow contact with the extended fingers following the initial contact with the heel of the open hand is essential to impart over spin if a hard hit ball is to stay within the court boundaries.

Coordination of Approach, Arm and Hand Movement, and Rotation of the Body

Body Mechanics

1. From a starting position away from the net at an approximate 45-degree angle, the spiker steps left, right, left, jump.
2. When the left foot touches the floor in the third step, the knee is bent in preparation for the jump. As the spring upward is taken, the right arm moves into its backswing. The right knee is brought up well in front of the body to add momentum to the jump.
3. At the maximum height of the jump the arm and hand complete their spiking motion with simultaneous body rotation.
4. From this elevated position squarely facing the net, the spiker drops to the floor on both feet.
   a. Bend the knees and land on the balls of the feet to absorb shock.
   b. Spring up slightly to regain balance and return to court position.

Coaching Suggestions

1. *The number of steps preceding the jump will be determined by the distance the spiker must travel from her court position to the set pass.* For purposes of initial introduction, however, three steps are desirable.
2. The take-off from the left foot is similar to that used by the basketball player taking a lay-up shot.
3. The slight spring upward after spiking will also aid in keeping her off the center line and out of the net.
4. Swing the arms upward directly overhead as the spring is taken after landing to help maintain body balance.

Drills

1. A simple drill to introduce the coordination of the approach, jump, and spike is diagrammed in Figure 5 (p. 21).
   a. The first experience should be planned to allow the spiker to experiment without the added psychological obstacle of the net so that she can be concerned with body movement and not possible contact with the net or concentration in order to avoid it.
   b. The line on the floor will suffice to give her an objective gauge of relative distance.

   c. She must be coached to jump straight upward and descend in approximately the same path rather than to jump forward in an arc toward the net.

   d. The slight spring from the floor after the spike can be emphasized to carry her upward and backward away from the line.

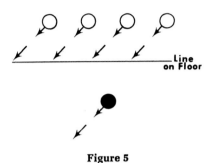

2. After she has become relatively proficient in this coordination, the spiker will want a more realistic game simulation. A basketball basket is usually accessible and offers an object to contact or an objective measurement of height on the jump. As diagrammed in Figure 6:

   Figure 5

   a. Each spiker in turn approaches, jumps, and strikes at the basketball net.

   b. The instructor stands about three feet behind the vertical plane of the back of the net with her arms extended overhead.

   c. She serves as a reminder of the net and can give individual coaching suggestions as each spiker participates in the drill (she can also move to avoid contact with the spiker!)

   d. The instructor should emphasize:

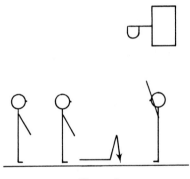

   Figure 6

     1. Beginning the approach close enough to the basket to allow for only three steps,

     2. A jump that is as straight upward and downward as possible,

     3. Landing on the balls of both feet with knees bent to absorb shock,

     4. An upward and backward spring terminating the spike.

Spike Across the Net

Body Mechanics

1. The instructor tosses the ball to *the desired position* which is approxi-

mately three feet from the net, approximately six feet above the net, and half way between spiker and instructor.
2. Approach and jump,
3. Arm and hand movement are performed with body rotation,
4. Land without unnecessary jar.

Coaching Suggestions

1. At this stage of learning the regulation height of the net is immaterial.
2. The important considerations are *correct body mechanics, timing in relation to another moving object,* and *SUCCESS.*
3. The instructor should lower the net to provide for these three essentials and *gradually raise the net as progress is made.*
4. Individual differences in ability are diverse, therefore homogeneous grouping is desirable and allows for more rapid progress.
5. The tossed ball representing the set pass should have no spin or as little as possible. A spinning ball is more difficult to spike and direct.
6. Points to emphasize in this progression are:
   a. Proper placement of the ball,
   b. The position of the spiker prior to the approach (her initial position should be approximately six feet from the net and approximately three feet from the side line),
   c. The diagonal approach *after the spiker has determined the direction of the set pass,*
   d. Starting the jump behind the ball so that it is contacted well in front of the body to allow for leverage and power.
7. The most common errors encountered at this stage are:
   a. Prior to the approach the spiker moves too close to the net so that she is approaching at an approximate 90-degree angle to the net instead of a 45-degree angle.
   b. Prior to the approach she moves so far away from the net that she has to take more than three steps and the ball drops out of position before she reaches it *or* so close that she leaves herself no approach and consequently reduced jumping power.
   c. She begins to move before she has determined where the set pass will be and must change direction or stop before jumping, which nullifies the advantage gained by an approach.
   d. She contacts the ball directly over her head which makes it impossible to do little other than push the ball and *pushing is illegal.*
   e. As she jumps following the approach, she lifts her arm upward with a relatively straight elbow *instead of moving it into the*

proper backswing position as described previously in the body mechanics section for the arm and hand movement. This is a very common and very serious error because (1) it drastically reduces power or (2) results in a push or throw. It is analogous to a bunt in softball: if the bat (the arm and hand in the spike) is not moved into a backswing position well away from the contact point, reduced hitting power results. So in essence, if the spiker does not move the arm into a full back swing position she "bunts" rather than spikes forcefully.

8. The coach should be aware that *at this time contact with the net and stepping over the center line are unimportant.* These two factors are already uppermost in the spiker's mind and added emphasis by the coach retards progress. As the spiker develops coordination, timing, and power these factors will then logically become important.

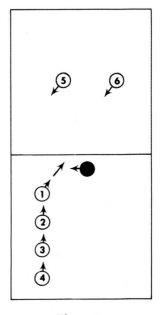

Figure 7

Drills

1. Figure 7 diagrams six spikers and the instructor.
   a. Each spiker hits two or three balls and rotates. Hitting several balls in succession aids the player to kinesthetically work through errors and make corrections.
   b. Those on the opposite side of the net recover the spiked balls and bounce them under the net to the instructor when she is ready. From this position she can give individual coaching.
   c. She may also have an experienced player toss the set pass and be free to supervise activity and give instruction on more than one court.
   d. After spiking, #1 becomes #6 and each player rotates one position.
2. Figure 8 shows a side view and Figure 9 a top view of a ball held at spiking position.
   a. This is excellent for the spiker having difficulty with timing. She may be letting the ball drop below net level before contacting it.
   b. This technique forces her to jump in order to contact the ball.

c. The angle of the ball holder's arm should be sufficient to prevent the spiker's contacting the umpire's stand if she should cross the net.
d. The ball is supported with one hand beneath the ball.
e. If an umpire's stand is not available a chair on top of a table, a self-supporting ladder, or some other substitution can be made.

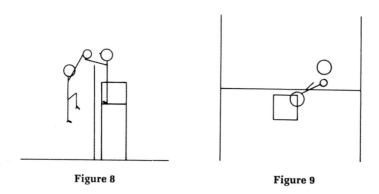

Figure 8   Figure 9

Spike a Set Pass

Body Mechanics

1. The set passer passes the ball to the desired position,
2. The spiker approaches and jumps,
3. Arm and hand movement with body rotation are executed,
4. She lands with flexed ankles and knees.

Coaching Suggestions

1. This situation strains the new-found confidence of the spiker, for the set passer is rarely as consistent with placement of the set pass as is the player merely tossing a ball.
2. There must be psychological rapport between the two players—successful performance by each one depends upon the other.
3. The coach may need to lower the net again temporarily, even though the spiker has progressed to the level of regulation net height in spiking a ball tossed into the proper position. The added set passer and the adjustments necessary to her presence may temporarily cause regression.
4. The coach should be cognizant of this and encourage the spiker

verbally in addition to lowering the net, and then raise it gradually as confidence and effectiveness develop.

Drills

1. The drill in Figure 10 provides excellent practice for both spiker and set passer.

   a. The ball is started by spiker #2 who tosses it into the air and executes an overhand pass to the set passer #1. (Spikers are black.)

   b. Set passer #1 sets the ball for spiker #1.

   c. Each spiker should hit two or three balls before rotating, since mistakes are more easily recognized and corrected if there is not a long waiting period between attempts.

   d. Spiker #3 should have several balls easily accessible so that they can be handed to spiker #2 to avoid delay.

   e. Set passer #3, recovering the spiked balls, should roll them under the net to spiker #3 at times when this does not interfere with the set passing and spiking.

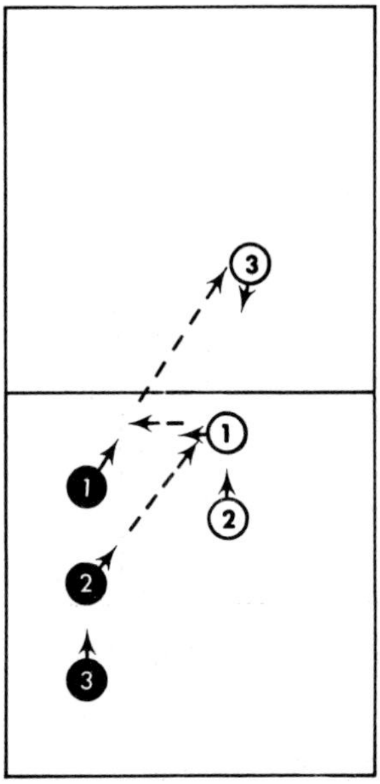

Figure 10

   f. Rotation of both spiking line and set passer line occurs simultaneously,

      1. Spiker #1 moves to a position behind spiker #3,
      2. Set passer #1 moves across the net,
      3. Set passer #3 moves to a position behind set passer #2.

   g. The recovery process is best delegated to the set passers because their function in the drill is less strenuous.

   h. This drill affords the coach an excellent opportunity to stress the interdependence of the players on a team.

      1. Without an accurate pass from the #2 spiker the set passer will be pulled out of desirable position and will be handicapped in her performance, thereby reducing the possibility of a "kill" by the spiker.

      2. A poor set pass resulting from lack of skill by the set passer will necessitate the spiker's getting the ball over the net the "best way she can" which, in a game situation, would mean that the opponents have an opportunity to take the offensive with no difficulty.

3. A poor performance by the spiker, even though she received a well-placed set pass, would put her team on the defensive in a game.

2. If space in the gymnasium is limited, players can perform the same drill from both sides of the net as diagrammed in Figure 11.

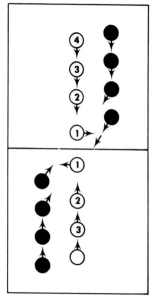

a. Players must learn that spikes should alternate—first from one side of the net and then the other.

b. Both sides never should spike simultaneously and *all players on the opposite side of the net should watch the spiker who is hitting* to avoid being struck by a spiked ball.

c. Recovery is made by any player on the opposite court and the ball need not be returned until it is spiked back.

The section which follows gives those errors which occur most often in the spiking progression and suggestions for their correction.

Figure 11

COMMON ERRORS	COACHING HINTS
1. The spiker "runs under" the ball, causing her to reach directly above or slightly behind her head to contact the ball; this results in drastic reduction of power and a pushing foul.	1. Wait until the set passer has actually contacted the ball and its direction can be determined before the approach is begun. Adjust length of the steps in proportion to distance to be covered.
2. The spiker is too close to the set passer and does not have an opportunity to approach, only to jump with consequent loss of timing and height.	2. Stay in position—approximately three feet from the side line and six feet from the net—until the set passer has contacted the ball. Have confidence in her ability and trust her to perform her job. Moving into the set passer's court position puts additional pressure on her.
3. The spiker contacts the ball with the palm and fingers instead of including the heel of the hand, causing loss of power or pushing or both.	3. a. The timing is off slightly and the jump is started too soon. Wait for the set pass until its direction is determined.
	b. Jump! Give a mental reminder each time the approach is begun—"jump high."

4. The spiker contacts the net.

4. The set pass should be farther from the net. The tall spiker can have the set pass closer than the short spiker. If the set pass is too close to the net to allow a follow-through directly toward the net, move the arm diagonally forward from the back swing position and follow through diagonally forward and to the side.

5. The spiker uses a "windmill" arm action which involves little or no movement of the elbow and contact with the ball while the body is in an approximate 90-degree angle to the net. This reduces power (though it may be useful in situations where the ball reaches the spiker directly from the set passer in a position as a back row player).

5. Approach the net on a diagonal rather than on a line parallel with the net. Jump from behind the ball and rotate the shoulders and hips as the forward swing of the arm is taken.

6. The spiker contacts the ball too far out to the right side as opposed to contacting it forward of the mid-line of the body directly in line with the shoulder. This reduces both power and ability to direct the line of flight of the spiked ball.

6. Jump from behind the ball. In the forward swing, the biceps are kept close to the ear and the hand travels forward over the head rather than to the right side of the head.

7. The spiker steps over the center line.

7. Practice jumping straight up instead of in a forward arc. Use a lift of the right knee and left arm to help gain an upward instead of a forward jump. Following the spike, bend the knees and spring in an upward direction, lifting the arms above the head.

8. A spiker who makes a powerful spike is so elated that she stands and admires the results instead of preparing for the possible recovery by the opponents.

8. The spiker should return to her court position immediately to be ready for the next play. The play is never complete until the ball hits the floor or ceiling or the referee declares the ball dead.

9. The spiker who makes one all-out effort right after another becomes depressed by a defensive team which keeps getting the ball back over the net.

9. If the spiker "gives up" she defeats herself. She should remind herself each time she jumps to put everything she has into the hit. **This** will be the one!

Advanced Power Spiking

The very highly-skilled power volleyball spiker (male and female) at national level competition uses an approach and jump that differ from those previously described.

Body Mechanics

1. The approach is directly forward toward the net, which eliminates the necessity of shoulder and hip rotation other than that which occurs as a result of moving the arm into its proper backswing position and then moving it forward.
2. This approach also makes it easier for the spiker to direct the spike to any part of the opponents' court by rotating the wrist and hand to point in the desired direction; conversely, the spiker taking a diagonal approach will find it easier to direct the spike straight forward, or to her right, than to her left. This direction of the spike is most advantageous in "playing the block" as discussed under *coaching suggestions* for formations utilizing four spikers and two set passers.
3. The jump preparatory to the spike is taken from both feet simultaneously:
    a. Approach straight forward with the number of steps necessary to cover the distance—preferably two or three.
    b. Jump forward onto both feet simultaneously.
    c. Crouch—bend the ankles, knees, hips, and back, move the arms downward and backward into a backswing position behind the back.
    d. Spring to a maximum height from both feet by extending all joints mentioned in *c*, swinging the left arm vigorously upward and outward, and moving the right arm and hand into its backswing position.
4. Otherwise mechanics for the advanced spike are the same as for the diagonal approach and one foot take-off.

Coaching Suggestions

1. The coach should be guided by the ability of her players and *strive to develop the maximum potentiality of each.*
2. If the player is capable of achieving enough height, she should be taught and encouraged to use the straight forward approach and two foot take-off.
3. The set pass must travel farther from the set passer so that it is directly in front of the spiker.

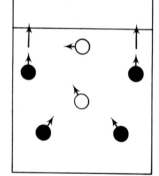

Figure 12

Illustration

Figure 12 illustrates the position of four spikers and two set passers and the approach direction of the spiker using a two foot take-off.

Playing the Block

It is to the advantage of the spiker to "play the block," which means that she hits the ball at an angle rather than straight forward into the block.

a. A ball spiked hard and straight forward will rebound into the spiker's court. Most of these spikes that are blocked back into the spiker's court hit the floor—and thus cause the loss of a point or the serve—because there is very little time for the spiker's teammates to judge the flight of the ball and make an effective recovery.

b. A ball hit at an angle rebounds at an angle in the opposite direction.

c. A ball spiked from the *side line* of the LF position and hit into the block at a right to left angle will in all probability rebound out of bounds, and the teammates of the spiker will not have to play the ball in order to win a point or the service.

d. A ball spiked from the *side line* of the RF position and hit into the block at a left to right angle will in all probability rebound out of bounds. (See Figure 13.)

e. It is for these reasons that advanced teams utilize set passes to and spikes from near the side lines. Set passes are occasionally made to the areas in between at opportune times to confuse the opposition by avoiding a rigid pattern of offense. This is used to great advantage by teams employing a 5 - 1 or 6 - 0 offense in which there are three spikers and one set passer on the front line.

f. Spiking at an angle rather than straight forward is accomplished by the spiker's turning her wrist at impact so that the palm faces in the desired direction with the follow-through in the direction of flight. (See the photographs of the U.S. vs Rumania page 67 and Japan vs USSR page 77.)

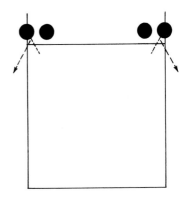

Figure 13

Illustration

The dotted lines in Figure 13 illustrate the flight of a spiked ball if the spiker uses the block to her advantage. The blockers deflect the ball out of bounds and the spiker's team wins point or side-out. This is the same principle utilized by a basketball player when she throws the ball against the backboard from a side angle so that it rebounds in the opposite direction into the basket.

Spiking the Second Hit

Players on the most advanced national and international teams have developed their ball handling skills to the point that the player receiving the ball coming over the net executes a set pass to one of the front row spikers who "kills" it from this first pass.

1. This is most advantageous as a change of pace, particularly if blockers are accustomed to pass, set pass, spike sequences. They therefore fail to set up an effective block.
2. A variation of this play is to have the spiker jump as though to spike and then pass while in the air to the other spiker who "kills" it. This diverts the blockers to the first spiker.
3. This is an advanced technique which requires advanced spiking and ball handling skills.

The Forward Set Pass

The set pass is an overhand pass which is used for a specific purpose and it is usually the second pass of the attack. This specific purpose is to achieve advantageous placement of the ball in a position close to and above the net so that the spiker can spike it successfully.

Body Mechanics

1. While awaiting the pass from a teammate:
   a. Assume a position about arm's length (approximately three feet) from the net at its center or near the side line in the LF or RF positions.
   b. Face the teammate who receives the ball coming over the net.
   c. *Watch the ball at all times.*
2. As the pass approaches:
   a. *Begin to turn the side directly to the net* (see Figures 14 and 15) and watch the ball over the shoulder as it arrives.
   b. Place the hands and arms in position:
      1. Elbows are bent and pointed slightly out to the sides,
      2. Hands are *above the upturned nose,*
      3. Fingers are extended but not stiff and are pointed diagonally upward and backward,
      4. The wrists are "cocked" so that the back of the hands form *almost* a 90-degree angle to the lower arms,
      5. Forefingers are approximately five inches apart,
      6. Thumbs are pointed inward, at an approximate 90-degree angle to the forefingers.
   c. BEND THE KNEES with the *feet parallel to the net* in a comfort-

able forward stride or side stride position with the weight on the balls of the feet.

3. Contact the ball with the terminal half of the *forefinger, second finger,* and *thumb* of each hand and simultaneously:

   a. Straighten the elbows upward and slightly forward to direct the ball in an arc toward the spiker,

   b. Push with the extended fingers and thumbs,

   c. Straighten the knees.

4. Follow through *upward* and *slightly forward,* holding this follow-through position of the hands and arms until the ball reaches the highest point of its arc.

5. Step backward so that there will be no physical or psychological interference with the spiker.

Coaching Suggestions

1. The desirable waiting position is at the net center and the distance from the net that the ball will be set (arm's distance or approximately three feet).

   a. This position may have to be changed because of the direction of the pass to the set passer.

   b. Waiting in the ideal location will give teammates an objective target toward which to pass.

2. This ideal position allows the set passer to be concerned with passing the ball in a *straight forward arc.*

3. A position farther from the net necessitates passing the ball in a diagonally forward arc, which is more difficult to judge and control.

4. It is imperative that the set passer watch the ball. If this requires turning the back toward the net:

   a. She remains facing the teammate passer until the ball is contacted by that player.

   b. As the ball travels toward the set passer she turns her feet and body to a 90-degree angle to the net and watches the ball approach over her shoulder. HER BODY IS FACING THE SIDE LINE.

   c. As the ball approaches she moves the hands and arms into position and bends the knees.

   d. *Do not turn the body as the ball is contacted.*

5. After the body has been turned to a 90-degree angle toward the net, necessary adjustment in floor position is made with sideward sliding steps.

6. DO NOT JUMP TO MEET THE BALL. Remain in a slightly crouched position until the fingers contact the ball.

a. The set pass does not require distance.

b. The set pass requires *accuracy*.

c. Jumping or extending the knees and elbows before contact will destroy accuracy and reduce potential power.

7. A spinning set pass is difficult to spike and control. The separation of the forefingers at contact with the ball will help in eliminating the spin. Actually, the ball is contacted on its "sides" and not directly behind it.

8. *The ideal height for a set pass is that elevation at which the spiker actually contacts the ball.* A ball travelling in an upward arc hesitates momentarily before descending. A spike contact at this moment when the ball is "suspended motionlessly" is much more easily spiked and controlled.

a. A ball set very high is moving at a rapid rate when it returns to the elevation of the spiker's contact.

b. The spiker's timing for a low set pass is delicate, requires an adjustment in the distance of her "waiting position" from the net, and absolute coordination with the set passer because of the reduction in time available for the approach, but the ultimate results are worth the drill and perseverance required.

c. This low set pass also gives the defense less time to position a blocker and establish other defensive positions.

d. High set passes are practically impossible in a gymnasium with low overhead clearance. Should a team have to play in such a gymnasium in a tournament situation, the striker and set passer could probably not adjust their timing in the time allotted.

e. Since the timing is so delicate in spiking a ball set at the "ideal height," most set passers and spikers will have to compromise between it and a very high set pass which is undesirable.

Illustrations

1. Figure 14 illustrates the position from which the CF set passer will contact the ball if the pass comes from a teammate at LF, LB, or CB positions (numbers indicate serving order). She could also set backward to the RF.

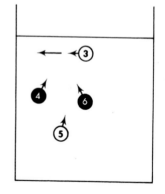

Figure 14

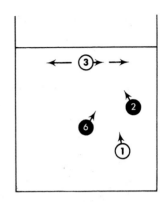

Figure 15

2. Figure 15 illustrates the position from which the CF set passer will contact the ball if the pass comes from a teammate at RF, RB, or an altered CB position. She may set to either the LF or RF position.

Drills

1. Figure 16 diagrams a set pass into the basketball net.
   a. The objective is to execute a set pass that will drop directly into the basket without hitting the rim.
   b. There should be just enough height in the arc to put the ball above the basket so that it can drop in.
   c. It is important that the set passer be close to the basket since the set pass requires accuracy and not distance. She should be no farther than five feet away.
   d. Set passer #4 tosses the ball up and executes an overhand pass to #1.
   e. Set passer #1 executes a set pass into the basket.
   f. Rotation occurs in a counterclockwise direction after #1 has passed two or three times in succession.

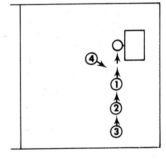

Figure 16

2. Figure 17 diagrams a simple and functional drill for practicing the set pass.
   a. Set passer #4 tosses the ball and executes an overhand pass to #1.
   b. Set passer #1 sets the ball at the proper location for a spike.
   c. Set passer #4, in addition to originating the play, acts as an objective target for #1 who is attempting to set the ball halfway between the two of them.
   d. Set passer #4 runs up and catches the ball.
   e. Rotation occurs in a counterclockwise direction after #1 has set two or three balls.

f. This is a good drill for set passers to use for warm-up purposes
while spikers spike against the wall.

The Backward Set Pass

Often in a game situation it is necessary
or advantageous for the set passer to set the
ball behind her rather than forward.

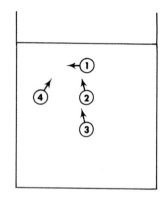

Occasions for Use

1. The teammate making the first pass of
the offensive play is in such a position
that the set passer must turn her back
to the spiker.
2. The set passer playing CF position and
facing the LF thinks it desirable to set to
the RF to disconcert the defensive team
which is expecting a spike from the LF.

Figure 17

Body Mechanics

1. Basically the mechanics are the same as for the forward set pass.
2. The differences are:
   a. *The body must be directly beneath the ball* in order to make a
   backward hit.
   b. The wrist has a greater flexion so that the back of the hand is at
   a 90-degree angle to the floor.
   c. The motion of hands and arms at contact is in an upward and
   backward direction.
   d. The *follow-through is upward and backward.*
   e. The back is arched so that the set passer can look directly upward.

Coaching Suggestions

1. This technique takes a great deal of practice because the set passer
is "blind" in terms of being able to see the spiker. It involves consid-
erable reliance upon the "feel" of the necessary distance the ball is
to travel.
2. If the set passer is passing backward to a RF spiker who uses the
diagonal approach the set pass must travel much farther than it does
ordinarily, because the spiker approaches to her right away from the
set passer and toward the sideline instead of moving toward the set
passer and the net.
3. As the pass approaches, the set passer should step forward, then

bend the knees to be sure she is directly under the ball.

Drill

Figure 18 diagrams a drill for practicing the backward set pass.

1. Spiker #3 passes the ball to set passer #1 at CF position.
2. Set passer #1 executes a backward set pass.
3. Spiker #1 spikes the ball across the net.
4. Set passer #3 recovers the ball and bounces it under the net to spiker #3.
5. After set passer #1 has executed two or three backward set passes she moves across the net to recover; set passer #2 moves to the net; set passer #3 moves to a position behind #2.
6. Spiker #1 then starts the ball, spiker #2 spikes, and spiker #3 moves to a position behind #1.

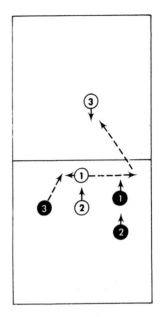

Figure 18

The section which follows outlines those errors which occur most often in set passing and presents suggestions for their correction.

COMMON ERRORS	COACHING HINTS
1. The ball is set too high and thus touches an overhead obstruction or is travelling at a rapid rate when it reaches a height to be contacted by the spiker.	1. Spikers must practice sufficiently to develop the timing required for low set passes.
2. The ball is set too close to the net. The spiker loses her potential power because of fear of touching the net or may actually commit a net foul.	2. The set pass should be about three feet away from the net. Short spikers must have the ball farther from the net than tall spikers.
3. The set passer is pulled out of position so that she must pass diagonally forward toward the net rather than passing parallel to the net.	3. Teammates must be drilled in **passing to a position**—one that is advantageous for the set passer. Until a team becomes accustomed to playing together the set passer should announce, "I'm setting," each time the ball comes over the net to remind each team member of her position at that time.

4. The set passer attempts to use an underhand motion. It is too difficult to place the ball with this type of pass.

4. Bend the knees deeply in a squat position with the knees widespread for balance in order to get under the ball for an overhand hit, or fall onto the knee pads.

5. The set passer extends arms and legs upward to meet the ball or jumps to meet it; this sacrifices accuracy and power.

5. It is imperative that the set passer **remain on the floor,** wait for the ball, and extend arms and knees as the ball is contacted without leaving the floor.

6. The set pass is spinning, which makes it difficult for the spiker to control.

6. The set passer should separate the forefingers so that the fingers contact the ball on its sides rather than directly behind it.

The Overhand Pass

The overhand pass probably is used more than any other technique in the game of volleyball. It must be mastered by any player who desires to play the game well. This technique allows the ball to be moved from one player to a teammate or over the net with more accuracy than any play.

Occasions for Use

1. A player uses the overhand pass to receive the service and send the ball to the set passer.
2. It is used to receive a spike.
3. It is used offensively to catch the defensive team out of position.
4. A set passer receiving a pass that is impossible to set uses the overhand pass to send the ball over the net.

Body Mechanics

1. Face the ball.
2. Move to a position that will allow the ball to approach in a position that is advantageous to its interception.
3. Just prior to contact:
   a. Elbows are bent,
   b. Hands are *above* and *slightly in front of* the upturned face,
   c. Fingers are straight but not stiff and are pointed diagonally upward and backward, forefingers approximately five inches apart,
   d. Thumbs are at an approximate 90-degree angle to the forefingers,
   e. The feet are in a comfortable forward stride or side stride,
   f. The knees are bent and the weight is on the balls of the feet.
4. Contact the ball with the terminal half of each forefinger, second finger, and thumb and simultaneously:

a. Straighten the elbows upward and forward to direct the ball in a forward arc,

b. Push with the extended fingers,

c. Straighten the knees.

5. Follow through upward and forward, holding this follow-through position of the hands and arms until the ball reaches the highest point of its arc.

6. If extra power is needed the passer can use a slight jump *with the follow-through.*

Coaching Suggestions

1. The player should be coached to watch the ball at all times, to determine its direction as soon as possible, and *move* to a position that will allow her to handle the ball with an overhand pass.

2. All moving should be completed *before the ball is contacted* so that the body is in its waiting position prior to contact.

3. The arc of the pass should be high enough to allow the intended receiver time to get in position to handle the ball.

4. The ball should drop in front of the intended receiver or directly over her head rather than behind her.

5. Unless the pass is an extremely long one, the passer should not jump with the follow-through because this to some extent destroys accuracy.

6. Extreme height on the pass is not necessary. There is the danger of overhead obstruction, and the higher the pass the more momentum it has on its flight downward.

7. Most balls could be handled with an overhand pass if the receiver would MOVE and bend the knees even if this meant squatting until heels and "backside" meet.

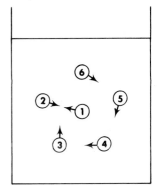

Figure 19

Drills

1. Figure 19 diagrams a drill for practicing the overhand pass.

a. Player #1 tosses the ball and executes an overhand pass to #2.

b. Player #2 returns the ball to #1 with an overhand pass.

c. The players forming the outside of the circle are moving clockwise.

d. Player #3 should be in the position previously occupied by #2 by the time the center player passes the ball back to that position.

e. The circle continues to move, with each player in turn executing an overhand pass.

f. The center passes the ball to the same position each time.

g. As a player nears the position from which she will contact the ball, she should face the center directly and use sideward sliding steps to assume her proper body position in relation to the ball.

h. It is imperative that the player in the outside of the circle who is to pass the ball do her moving *before contact;* she should determine the ball's direction and be *waiting* in the proper position so that her body is not moving when she actually contacts the ball.

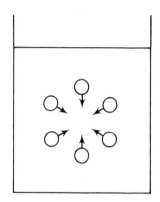

2. Figure 20 diagrams another drill for practicing the overhand pass and movement into correct position.

Figure 20

a. Any player tosses the ball and executes an overhand pass.

b. The players are all moving in a clockwise direction with sideward sliding steps.

c. The player nearest the ball after the first pass slides into a position under the ball and executes an overhand pass to any other player.

d. Again it is important that the player who is to execute the pass determine the ball's direction, move to an advantageous position, and be stationary at the time of contact.

COMMON ERRORS	COACHING HINTS
1. The passer uses some technique other than the overhand pass.	1. MOVE! The player should watch the ball at all times, determine its direction and speed, and be in the proper position in readiness when the ball arrives.
2. The passer fails to bend the knees adequately.	2. With foresight, concentration, and repeated practice the player will be able to handle most balls with the overhand pass. Maximum knee flexion should be utilized on low balls. Sliding forward onto the kneepads will enable the player to execute the overhand pass in many difficult situations.
3. The passer places the ball poorly in relation to the set passer.	3. In the excitement of play it is easy to forget position and team strategy. The player should know the desired desti-

nation before the ball gets to her. A verbal reminder by the set passer or some other player each time the ball crosses the net is helpful. In the learning stages it is helpful if the set passers wear colored pinnies to distinguish them.

The Backward Pass

Occasions for Use

1. A player with her back to the net is executing the third hit which must go to the opponents' court.
2. A set passer receives a pass which is too high for her to set accurately and she must "save" the ball by getting it over the net.
3. A player "backing up" a teammate and moving away from the net with speed which does not allow her an opportunity to face the net must pass behind her.

Body Mechanics

1. The mechanics are essentially the same as for a backward set pass.
2. In situation #2 above she may have to jump in order to contact the ball.
3. In situation #3 above she will be unable to get in the desirable stationary position and must contact the ball while she is moving, which will reduce control of the ball.

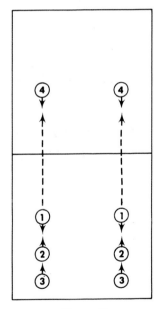

Coaching Suggestions

1. It is important that the *fingers point diagonally backward over the head.* If they point away from the body the movement is essentially an underhand one which is more likely to result in "throwing the ball."
2. The player should realize that this technique is not as effective as the forward pass and should be used only in emergencies.
3. The body should not turn toward the net

Figure 21

as the technique is executed. The follow-through should be completed before the passer turns to determine whether her efforts were successful.

Drill

Figure 21 diagrams a drill for practicing the backward pass.
1. Player #2 tosses the ball and executes an overhand pass to #1.
2. Player #1 executes the backward pass.
3. Player #4 recovers the ball and rolls it under the net to #2.
4. After #1 has executed the backward pass two or three times the line rotates with #1 moving across the net, #2 moving forward to execute the backward pass, and #4 moving to a position behind #3.

The Offensive Pass

Occasions for Use

1. An offensive player detects an uncovered area of the defensive team's court and uses the offensive pass to "catch them out of position."
2. An offensive player notes that the defensive team is temporarily off guard—its members are waiting for the ball to reach the spiker—and passes offensively.
3. A player is the third member of the team to receive the ball and is unable to spike or the preceding pass was not an adequate set pass; she passes the ball to a position where it will be most difficult for the opponents to return.

Body Mechanics

1. The mechanics are essentially the same as for the overhand pass.
2. The factors that differ are:
   a. The body must be *well behind* the ball to allow for additional power.
   b. The hands should contact the ball after it has dropped a bit lower than for a set pass.
   c. The follow-through is *primarily forward* and slightly upward.

Coaching Suggestions

1. All players should be constantly aware of the need to detect a lack of alertness on the part of the defensive team.
2. Do not telecast the intention to pass offensively—this must be a surprise movement.

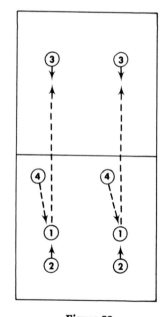

Figure 22

3. An extremely high pass will defeat its purpose—the defensive team can recover court position in the time made available by a high pass.

Drill

Figure 22 diagrams a drill to practice the offensive pass.
1. Player #4 at the net tosses the ball and executes an overhand pass.
2. Player #1 executes an offensive pass across the net.
3. Player #3 recovers the ball and bounces it under the net to #4.
4. After #1 has executed two or three offensive passes, the line rotates with #4 moving across the net, #1 moving to the net to start the ball, and #3 moving to a position behind #2.

The "Dink" or "Soft Spike"

Occasions for Use

1. The spiker uses less power occasionally to vary the pace of the game and to confuse the opposition—she can often win a point or side out against a proficient blocker who keeps returning hard hit spikes. A "soft spike" tends to hit the block and drop into the blockers' court if they have not reached over the net to do the blocking.
2. The "dink" is used to hit *over* or *around* blockers to vacant spots.
3. A powerful spiker can fake a "kill" and then "dink" the ball over or to the side of the blocker when she jumps.
4. The spiker can use a "dink" to play a set pass that is so close to the net that she cannot spike without touching the net.

Body Mechanics

1. Approach the net and jump exactly the same as for a power spike.
2. The ball can be contacted in one of several ways:
   a. The *heel of the open hand* can be used.
      1. The hand is in the same position as for contacting a power spike: hand open and wrist "cocked" so that the fingers are back to form almost a 90-degree angle to the forearm.
      2. To "dink" instead of hitting with power, *no wrist snap forward occurs.*
      3. The follow-through is *very short* (a light tap) in the direction of intended flight.
      4. The fingers never touch the ball.
   b. The *clenched fist can be used.*
      1. The ball is contacted with the "face" of the fist—the heel of the hand and the second knuckles of the fingers.

2. The wrist is straight, not "cocked."
3. The follow-through is *very short* in the direction of intended flight.

c. The *ends of the stiffened fingers* can be used.
1. Bend the wrist forward so that the tips of the fingers point toward the net.
2. "Punch" the ball with the fleshy ends of the fingers.
3. The follow-through is *very short* in the direction of desired flight.

Coaching Suggestions

1. The "dink" or "soft spike" can be particularly devastating if the "cover" behind the block is relaxed or has not been established. The spiker must observe the defensive team's position to detect such opportunities.
2. The spiker must be sure that she hits the ball "cleanly" and does not carry or push it because officials call these plays very sternly. The more strict the officiating the more dangerous it is to use the fingers in preference to the fist.
3. The spiker should use the identical approach and preliminary arm actions for a power spike because:
a. The defense must not be warned,
b. She can change her mind in the air if the defensive actions warrant it.

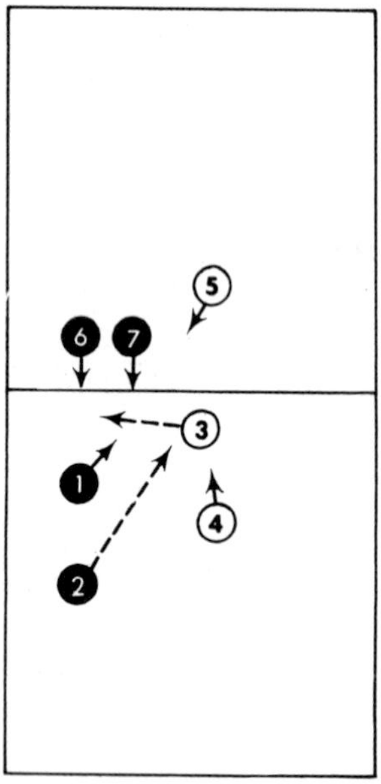

Drill

Figure 23 diagrams a drill for practicing the "dink."
1. Player #2 executes an overhand pass to set passer #3.
2. Set passer #3 executes a set pass.
3. Spiker #1 executes the "dink" either behind or to the side of blockers #6 and #7.
4. Player #5 recovers the ball and bounces it under the net to player #2.

Figure 23

The Service

The service is the technique used by the right back player to put the ball into play. The rules state that only the serving team may score a point. This is very important from the standpoint of the psychology of playing. The receiving of the service gives a team its first opportunity to assume the offensive role in a rally, but *it cannot score from this offensive maneuver.* Many teams seem to operate in reverse of this principle. Some of their most diligent and enthusiastic psychological and physical endeavors are manifested in attempts to win the service from their opponents, but they seem to "lose their fire" when they have succeeded in recovering the service. *If there is any time that concerted effort is very important, it is when a team has the service.*

A player or coach may praise one type of service over another, but there is one basic principle—*a good service is one that goes over the net into the opponents' court.* Some services are more difficult to receive than others and should be utilized, provided they can be controlled. The server must first and foremost recognize the fact that her team cannot possibly score if she fails to get the ball into the opponents' court. The good service therefore is one that can be utilized with 100 percent accuracy.

Four types of service will be discussed. The underhand service is the easiest to master but is also the easiest for the opposing team to receive and convert into an attack. The sidearm service is a little more difficult to master but has some advantages over the underhand service because it is more difficult to receive. The overhead service can be a very valuable *offensive weapon* but is the most difficult to perform and control. The floater service is a variation of the overhead service.

The Underhand Service

Body Mechanics

1. Assume a stance anywhere behind the end line within the serving area.
   a. The feet are in a forward stride position, left foot forward (if the server is right-handed).
   b. The body is at an approximate 45-degree angle to the net (or slightly less).
   c. The left foot is far enough away from the end line to allow the server to step without getting on or over the end line.
   d. The knees are slightly flexed and the body weight is on the balls of the feet.
   e. The body is bent slightly forward from both waist and hip; eyes are on the ball.
   f. The left arm is dropped forward relatively straight at the elbow; the ball is supported by the upturned left palm which is slightly forward of the bottom of the ball; the ball itself is held about 12 inches in front of the left toe.

2. A backswing is taken with the right arm and body:
   a. The arm moves straight back from the end line, not in a circular motion around the body (the right arm movement resembles the pendulum-like movement of a grandfather clock).
   b. The body weight shifts to the right foot but the left hand maintains its same position with the ball, which means that as the body shifts backward the left arm is abducted at the shoulder to allow the ball to maintain its same position.

3. After the backswing these movements occur simultaneously:
   a. The right arm starts its swing straight forward,
   b. The left foot takes a small step forward,
   c. The body weight begins to be transferred from the right to the left foot,
   d. The hips and shoulders rotate so that the center of the body faces the net.

4. Contact the ball.
   a. The ball is contacted underneath and slightly behind its center bottom.
   b. The ball is batted from the left hand, which remains in its initial position.
   c. At this instant knees, hips, and waist are fully extended.
   d. The position of the right hand at contact may be either:
      1. A clenched fist with the ball batted with the flat second knuckle and heel of the hand (thumb extended beside the forefinger);
      2. An open hand with the ball batted by the *heel of the hand* with the extended and firm fingers aiding in giving direction to the service.
   e. The right elbow is extended and the leverage comes from the shoulder.

5. Follow through:
   a. The right arm continues in its pendulum-like motion straight toward the net and slightly upward,
   b. The eyes and head follow the ball,
   c. The right foot swings forward and the server *moves rapidly to her court position.*

Coaching Suggestions

1. If the desired direction of the service is not straight forward, this change is accomplished by the following alterations:
   a. A hit to the left is made possible by additional hip and shoulder

rotation so that at contact the center of the body is facing left (the line of intended ball flight) and the right arm follow-through is in that direction.
   b. A hit to the right is made possible by less hip and shoulder rotation so that at contact the center of the body is facing slightly right and the right arm follow-through is in that direction.
2. Accuracy is drastically reduced if the ball is tossed with the left hand instead of batted from the hand.
3. Servers who hit the ball too high and have difficulty getting distance need to:
   a. Hit behind and under the ball rather than directly beneath it,
   b. Apply the contact pressure forward and upward as opposed to hitting primarily upward,
   c. Use leverage from the shoulder rather than the elbow,
   d. Hold the ball lower with the left hand so that it is difficult to hit directly beneath the ball.

The Sidearm Service

Body Mechanics

1. Assume a stance behind the end line within the service area.
   a. The feet are in a side stride position.
   b. The body is at an approximate 90-degree angle to the net.
   c. The left foot is far enough away from the end line to allow the server a step without getting on or over the end line.
   d. The knees are slightly flexed and the body weight is on the balls of the feet.
   e. The body is relatively upright; eyes are on the ball.
   f. The left arm is extended forward; the ball is supported by the upturned left palm which is slightly forward of the bottom of the ball; the ball itself is about waist height directly in front of the left toe; the left arm is fully extended at the elbow.
2. A backswing is taken with the right arm and body:
   a. The arm is bent at the elbow and the hand moves backward in a slight semicircular movement on a plane level with the ball,
   b. The body weight shifts to the right foot; the hips and shoulders rotate to the right, but the left hand maintains its same position with the ball.
3. After the backswing these movements occur simultaneously:
   a. The right arm starts its swing forward from the shoulder with a straightening of the elbow,

    b. The left foot takes a very small step toward the net,

    c. The body weight begins to be transferred from the right to the left foot,

    d. The hips and shoulders rotate so that the center of the body faces in a direction parallel to the end line.

4. Contact the ball.

    a. The ball is contacted from behind and slightly underneath.

    b. The ball is batted from the left hand, which remains in its initial position.

    c. The knees, hips, and waist have rotated on a plane with their original stance—the knees do not extend at contact.

    d. The position of the right hand at contact may be either:

        1. A clenched fist with the ball batted with the flat second knuckle and heel of the hand (thumb extended beside the forefinger),

        2. An open hand with the ball batted by the heel of the hand with the extended and firm fingers helping give direction to the service. This open-handed position will allow the server to impart more spin, which makes the ball more difficult to receive.

    e. The right elbow is extended and the leverage comes from both the shoulder and the extension of the elbow which had been flexed in the backswing.

5. Follow-through:

    a. The right arm continues its swing forward and upward, terminating at a position pointing toward the net,

    b. The shoulders and hips continue their rotation and point forward toward the net,

    c. The feet remain firmly planted on the floor,

    d. The eyes follow the flight of the ball.

6. After the ball has been contacted and is well on its way, the player moves rapidly into her court position.

Coaching Suggestions

1. This service can be difficult to receive if the open hand is used to contact the ball, because a side spin can be imparted which makes it difficult for the receiver—it tends to rebound from her fingers at an angle.

2. The server should take her time so that she is ready psychologically and kinesthetically. She should think positively—the service *will* be good.

3. Service from behind that part of the service area closest to the center of the court leaves less margin of error and the center forward and center back players temporarily screen the service.

The Overhead Service

This service when perfected can be a valuable offensive weapon! It is the most difficult for opponents to receive and control.

Body Mechanics

1. Assume a stance behind the end line:
   a. The body faces the net squarely with the knees flexed slightly and the body weight on both feet.
   b. The left toe is just behind the end line; the right foot is a comfortable distance behind; the feet are hip width apart.
   c. The ball is supported with the fingers and thumb of the cupped left hand—directly in front of the right toe and right shoulder—with the air valve on the bottom.
2. The ball is tossed and a backswing is taken with the right arm and body simultaneously:
   a. The left arm pushes the ball upward and follows through to a position directly under the ball.
   b. The ball is tossed to the height where the server wishes to contact it with the right hand—about a foot higher than the head and six to eight inches in front of the body.
   c. The right arm bends at the elbow, the right hand is open, the wrist is cocked, the hand moves to a position behind the head, and the elbow points forward and sideward of the mid-line of the body.
   d. The body rotates at the hips and shoulders to allow the body weight to shift to the right foot.
   e. The eyes remain on the ball at all times.
3. After the backswing these movements occur simultaneously:
   a. The right arm starts its swing forward and slightly upward,
   b. The body weight begins to be transferred from the right to the left foot,
   c. The hips and shoulders begin to rotate so that the center of the body will face the net.
4. Contact the ball.
   a. The ball is contacted at 4:00 on its imaginary clock face with the heel of the open hand and then a vigorous snap of the wrist brings the extended fingers over the ball to impart top spin. This is the same hand action as for a spike except that the contact point on the ball differs.
   b. The right elbow is fully extended.
   c. The right hand is *directly in front of the right shoulder* and in front of the body (about 1:00 in the arm swing).

    d. The body weight is on the left foot and the knees are extended.

5. Follow through:

    a. The right arm continues to swing straight forward toward the net in line with the right shoulder and terminates in a position parallel to the floor with the fingers pointing downward.

    b. Following the wrist snap, the wrist is completely flexed.

6. After the ball is well on its way to the net, the player moves rapidly to her court position.

Coaching Suggestions

1. A stance to the left side of the service area will accomplish two objectives:

    a. The center back and center forward teammates act as a screen for the server, thus giving the opposition less time to watch the flight of the ball and move in line with its flight, a position they desire.

    b. This position allows the server to send the service toward the right, center, or left of the opponents' court with less margin of error.

2. The toss by the left hand should send the ball to the height where contact is desired.

    a. This allows the ball to be momentarily "dead" or suspended between its upward and then downward flight.

    b. A high toss necessitates waiting for the ball to descend and a moving target is more difficult to hit.

    c. This toss is very similar to a toss for the tennis service.

3. It is most important that:

    a. The original stance and the position at contact be facing the net.

    b. The contact is made with the flat heel of the hand and then the extended fingers of the hand.

4. A vigorous wrist snap at contact and bringing the extended fingers down over the ball impart top spin.

5. Both feet should maintain contact with the floor until after the ball is well on its way to the net.

6. Do not step into the court with the left foot before the ball is contacted.

7. This technique is very similar to the catcher's throw to the pitcher in softball except that the player is not in a squat position.

8. The player should have confidence in her ability and think positively with each service.

The Floater Service

The floater is a variation of the overhead service and differs from it in that there is no spin and its flight weaves because of the motion of the air valve. The weaving motion makes it difficult for the defending player to line up with the ball's flight and this makes it difficult to get off a good pass to the set passer. The floater service serves very advantageously as a "change of pace" technique.

The only differences in execution are:
1. The air valve is in front of the ball on the toss.
2. The right wrist is straight rather than cocked on the backswing and at contact.
3. The right hand is cupped slightly so that contact is made with the flat heel of the hand and the flat pad of the terminal knuckle of the fingers.
4. The right arm does not follow through after contact but is pulled backward sharply. This withdrawal is similar to that for popping a whip.

Drill

Players station themselves behind the end lines of the court and serve; therefore no additional retrievers are needed.

COMMON ERRORS OF SERVING	COACHING HINTS
1. The server hitting underhand gets too much height and not enough distance.	1. The left hand holds the ball low and well forward of the body because this position demands that the ball be hit forward as well as upward. Contact the ball at "four o'clock" on the imaginary clock face.
2. The server hits into the net.	2. CONCENTRATE. The server should not rush into the serve. Take a deep breath. Think positively.
3. The server hitting overhead sends the ball out of the court over the end line.	3. Snap the wrist vigorously at contact, slapping the extended fingers down over the ball in order to impart top spin. Follow through, with the wrist completely flexed, until the arm is parallel to the floor. (This hint **does not** apply to the floater service.)

Service Placement

After the player can get the service into the opposing court consistently she should become concerned with its placement within that

court. Advantageous service placement will be instrumental in causing
a poor series of plays by the receiving team. This weak play by the receiving team will enable the serving team to take the offensive role and
score. Several factors should be taken into consideration in determining
the most advantageous placement.

1. The best placement is to a weak opposing passer, if the team has one.
2. If the opponents position their back line players well back into the
   court for receiving, a low service which drops into mid-court is indicated, because this will require an underhand hit which is difficult to
   control and may result in a lifting foul.
3. A service placement to the right back position is desirable if there is
   a weaker spiker in the right forward position. This placement will get
   the set passer's back to her left forward spiker; thus the set passer
   must execute a backward set pass to the left forward which is more
   difficult than the forward set pass or set to the "off side" of the
   weaker spiker in the right forward position.
4. If the receiving center forward set passer stands well back from the
   net a service placement to her will make it difficult for her to set the
   ball well.

OFFENSIVE FORMATIONS

Every coach dreams of having six players on the court who can spike,
block, and set pass equally well. This would be ideal, but it rarely exists.
Consequently, most coaches resort to training some players to be mainly
spiking players and others to be set passers. Most teams will also have
one or more set passers who are literally too short in stature to block.
Formations are determined somewhat by the abilities of a particular
group of girls.

All spikers should be drilled in set passing because they often must
set the ball to a spiking teammate and are more valuable team players
if they can do so. Often a spiker is so accustomed to spiking automati-
cally that should the occasion arise when she receives the ball to make
the second hit and could advantageously set pass to a spiking teammate
on the front row, she doesn't even think of the possibility.

Another important possibility is to pair the best spiker and the best
set passer and to have an effective server in position while they are in
the spiking position. A good spiker is helpless if she never gets a set pass
and the good set passes are wasted if given to an ineffective spiker. If the
best spiker and set passer are in the spiking position and the server
makes a serving error, they are then utilized to win the service back
instead of making points.

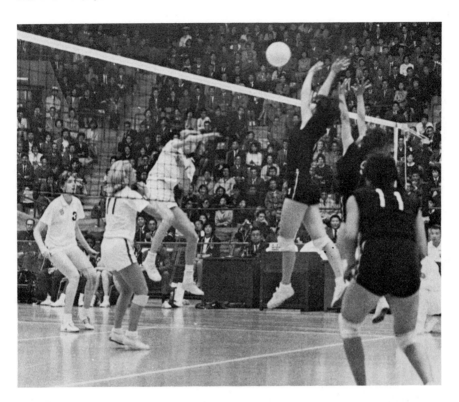

Komazawa Volleyball Court, Tokyo, October 21, 1964. Jean K. Gaertner of the United States spikes the ball for the 15th and final point to beat Korea in three straight sets (15 - 7, 15 - 13, 15 - 13). Match scores differ in International Rules.

This is a good illustration of a "cluster" around the spiker and the blockers to cover "vital areas." (Courtesy of Compix)

This also clearly illustrates the follow-through position of the spiker's arm, a multiple block, and position of the blockers' arms and hands.

It is to be emphasized at the outset that a good volleyball team is made up of good ball handlers. Any offensive system is dependent upon the consistency of individual, basic ball handling techniques. A sophisticated system of offense is dependent upon these basics. Most practice time of necessity centers upon the efficient first pass, set, and court coverage. Each team member must know the strengths and weaknesses of her teammates and coordinate their efforts; without coordination, the opponents have no real problem if they know what they are doing. Trust and faith in teammates by each team member is necessary to keep the group functioning as a team; if they don't do this, they usually beat themselves. Systems of offensive play are chosen to correspond with the abilities of a given group. Several possibilities follow.

A Basic Formation and Coverage of Vital Areas

This is the least complicated system of offense and is useful with an inexperienced team which is learning the mechanics of team play for power volleyball.

1. The CF is the set passer on every play.
2. The LF and RF players are spikers.
3. The CB backs up front row players and sets to one of the spikers if the LB or RB cannot pass the ball all the way to the CF set passer.

The main advantage is that players do not have to "switch" from one position to another which can be distracting for inexperienced players. It also gives all players experience in spiking and set passing to aid in their appreciation of various team responsibilities. Its simplicity is an advantage. The disadvantage is that all players cannot spike effectively even though the basic team work up to that point is good; this tends to discourage the "spiker" and the team.

Illustration

1. Figure 24 illustrates the basic "W" formation of the players other than the CF. The ball comes over the net to the LB who then passes it to the CF who executes a set pass to the LF (or backward to the RF).
2. The dotted line in Figure 25 shows the ball crossing the net to be received by the LB player.
   a. All players face the ball at all times.
   b. Player #1 moves immediately to a position to back up #5 as soon as she de-

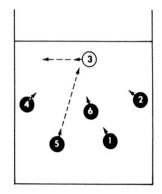

Figure 24

termines that the ball is going in that direction.

c. All other players take one or more steps in that direction.

3. Figure 26 shows the court position following the play in Figure 25 where the ball was passed from #5 to set passer #3 and spiked by the LF.

a. Note that there is a cluster of players around the spiker.

b. This formation provides good coverage for *a blocked ball which must be considered every time the ball is spiked.*

c. If the blockers send the ball back over the net the space must be covered.

d. If the block does not send the ball back immediately, then players *move out of this cluster* and prepare to receive the spike.

e. Good volleyball players keep moving.

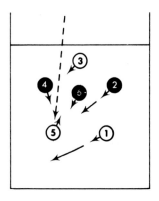

Figure 25

Drill

These formations for a basic offense and coverage of vital areas should be practiced repeatedly until they become automatic. A simple drill involves having a player across the net toss the ball to a position. The player in that position executes an overhand pass

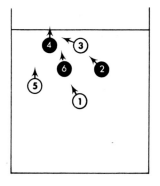

Figure 26

to the set passer; the set passer sets the ball up and the spiker hits. On *every hit every player should move toward the ball handler*—the distance is determined by the particular court position. The set passer and spiker will not move as far as the other players. The coach stands in a position where she can see all players clearly. On any play where a player or players are not moving into the proper position she should stop play immediately and point out the inadequacy—actually place the team members in the proper relationship to other players. It is a good practice to have players hold the position they occupied at the exact moment of the spiker's contact of the ball in order to give them an opportunity to see if they actually moved where they thought they did.

Have the team receive two to four balls and then rotate so that each player will become familiar with the responsibility of each court position. Several plays in the same position give a girl the opportunity to correct an error after she is aware of it.

Coaching Suggestions

1. All players should have experience in spiking and set passing even though they specialize in one technique; game situations do not allow one player to perform only her specialty.
2. Even short set passers can spike, though they will not get the same height on the jump or be able to hit directly downward into the opponents' court.
3. Spikers should be drilled in set passing to a spiking teammate in all situations where they occupy the RF and LF positions. This can be very confusing for the defensive team. The spiker who is alert to this particular situation will be a much more valuable player.
4. For greater team effectiveness, pair the most skilled spiker and set passer.
5. Figures 24–26 diagram vital offensive formations.
    a. Each player must become familiar with the responsibility of each court position.
    b. Each must understand that good court position necessitates *constant move-ment* and watching the ball at all times. Though the player's direct vision is focused on the ball, her peripheral vision allows her to see the position of teammates and opponents.

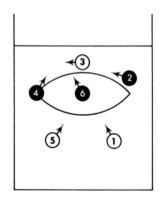

Figure 27

6. After the service is received, *the CB is no longer a back row player.*
    Her duty is to move in to cover all three players on the front row. This is the most vital area of the court and more balls hit the floor in this area than in any other. Figure 27 gives an idea of her court coverage *after the serve.* Should the service go to the CB position, she passes to the set passer on the front row and then moves to this area.
7. The team may feel that the formation in Figure 27 leaves the back court without adequate protection. One must weigh advantages and disadvantages. The team will have an opportunity to defend itself successfully with this formation *more often* than it will when exposing this vital area. *No defense is successful all the time* against a good power volleyball team.

The 4 - 2 System of Offense

There is great advantage for players in rules that permit players to "switch" or exchange positions on the court after the ball is served. In the 4 - 2 system there are always two spikers on the front line. This is advantageous because:

    a. Four spikers can be utilized in the game (even though the two on the back line cannot come forward of the spiking line to spike, they will be used when they rotate to the front line).

    b. The two spikers on the front line can move in order to be in the proper relationship to the set passer.

    c. There are always two spikers at the net. This can be confusing to the defense and there is always the possibility that one player may be "off" her game and not functioning efficiently.

    d. Some set passers are too short to block effectively and a spiker teammate on the front line can move out of position to do so.

    e. Team members know that the pass to the set passer always goes to the CF position and there is less likely to be confusion on pass direction.

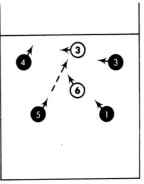

Figure 28

The following diagrams will give the teacher a visual picture of some of these formations.

1. Figure 28 diagrams a formation with four spikers and two set passers. A ball coming over the net is received by spiker #5 and passed to set passer #3 who may set to spiker #4 or behind her to spiker #2.

2. Figure 29 shows court position after one rotation from Figure 28. They are positioned to receive the service.

    a. Set passer #2 changes her court position to assume the CF position *as soon as the ball has been contacted on the service.*

    b. This is accomplished by having spiker #3 occupy the court position that she will use as a base for the ensuing

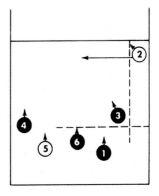

Figure 29

rally; that is, she is the spiker on the right side of the court. Before the service is contacted set passer #2 is very close to the side line so that only she has to change her position.

   c. The solid line and arrow indicate the movement and position of set passer #2.

   d. This is desirable because set passer #2 should not be involved in receiving the service, and she can move into position as the receiver is getting ready to field the service.

   e. This position is legal as long as the feet of players #2 and #3 and of #3 and #6 do not overlap on the floor. (The dotted lines indicate this lack of overlap which makes the positioning legal.

   f. Player #2 must return to her serving order position at the end of the rally until the next service is contacted. She then repeats the "switch" on each service until her team rotates.

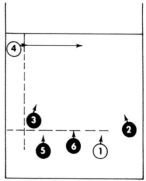

Figure 30

3. Figure 30 diagrams court position after one rotation from Figure 29. Set passer #4 then "switches" to occupy the center position for setting. This is the same process as diagrammed in Figure 29 except that it is on the opposite side of the court. Utilization of this "switching" process allows the team to maintain two spikers on the front row at all times—one on each side of the set passer. The feet of #4 and #3 and of #3 and #6 cannot overlap.

Coaching Suggestions

1. Spikers must be drilled in spiking a set pass coming from either the right or the left, though it is much more difficult for the right-handed spiker to spike a set pass from her left side (the "off side").

2. Set passers must be drilled in set passing backward as well as forward.

3. Set passers must understand that from the standpoint of body mechanics *the right handed spiker must be allowed to run straight forward or diagonally to her right.* Running left will force the spiker into an awkward position from which she cannot hit effectively.

4. The set pass to the spiker in the RF position will usually be a longer pass because of the condition described in suggestion #3.

5. If the set passer is not consistent with her passing to the RF position, the spiker might stand closer to the set passer so that she is able to

run straight forward or right instead of having to run to her left preparatory to spiking.

6. If the team uses the starting line diagrammed in Figure 28, the two best spikers should occupy serving positions #2 and #5. The spikers occupying these positions spike twice from the LF position and once from the RF position; the other two spikers spike once as LF and once as RF because of the switching.

7. Stress with the team that *all passes to the set passer go to the CF position.*

8. All players must remember to be in their serving order every time the ball is served to avoid being out of position and losing a point or the service. This sometimes presents a problem because of the switching of a set passer and a spiker.

9. It is simple for the set passer on the front row to determine her proper position by locating the other set passer. These two players are always opposite each other—CF and CB, or opposite corners (LF and RB, RF and LB).

10. The "switching" set passer should *move immediately after the server's hand* contacts the ball so that she is ready for her play.

11. Players may stand as close together as they desire as long as their feet do not overlap in their relative positions.

12. Note in Figures 29 and 30 (pp. 55, 56) that the set passer is close to the side line and close to the net. She moves to the CF position as soon as the server's hand contacts the ball. The spiker is back away from the net to be in position to receive the service and to avoid contact with the moving set passer. As soon as the set passer moves, both the CF set passer and the spikers are in desirable positions for the next play. The set passer should always attempt to be that distance from the net at which the ball will be set and the spiker needs an approach distance.

13. This four-spiker formation is very advantageous for the set passer.
    a. Regardless of which side of her body she has toward the net as a result of the first pass, there is always a spiker in front of her.
    b. Though she should be able to pass backward, some passes are difficult to get under in order to accomplish this.
    c. If she recognizes that one spiker is not being effective against the opposition she can utilize the other.
    d. If the defense is setting up effectively against the stronger spiker, she can set occasionally to the other to keep the defense guessing from where the spike will come.

14. The basic idea described in Figure 26 (p. 53) relative to covering the vital area of the court on a spike by a teammate must be observed. This "cluster" of players is necessary should the spiker be blocked

and the block rebound into the spiker's court. If this does not happen, then the players *move rapidly* into a different formation to receive the opponents' play.

The 5 - 1 System of Offense

This means that there are five spikers and one set passer on a team.

Mechanics

1. If the set passer is on the front line, her movements are the same as for the 4 - 2 offense. She "switches" if necessary to be in the CF position for set passing. She may set to the spiker in front of or behind her. So, when the set passer's serving position is on the front line, the team uses the basic 4 - 2 offensive pattern with two spikers.
2. If the set passer's serving order position places her on the back row after the serve, she moves to a position on the front row to be able to set to the left, center, or right forward spiker.
3. This means that fifty percent of the time the offense operates with two spikers and fifty percent of the time with three spikers on the front line.

Illustrations

Figure 31 diagrams the movement of the RB set passer to the front line setting position and the approach direction for the three front line spikers.

Figure 32 diagrams the movement of the CB set passer and the three spikers.

Figure 33 shows the movement of the LB set passer and the three spikers.

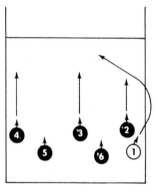

Figure 31

Coaching Suggestions

1. Players must be in their serving order positions for the service. At *contact of the ball* on the service, the set passer *moves rapidly* to her position. SHE NEVER RECEIVES THE SERVICE.
2. The spiker receiving the service makes a *controlled pass* high enough to give the set passer time to assume her position.
3. Figures 31 and 32 show the set passer positioned so that two right handed

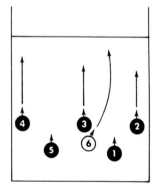

Figure 32

spikers are spiking from their "on side" because the set pass reaches them from their right.

4. When the set passer contacts the ball, *all three spikers make their approach and jump.* The primary advantage of this formation is *deception*—the defense does not know where the spike will come from and are thereby delayed in setting up the block.

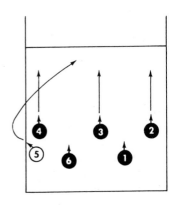

Figure 33

5. The center spiker makes her approach *as soon as the set passer contacts the ball;* if it comes to her, it will be low and reduces the approach time. The outside spikers start their approach *after the ball leaves the hands of* the set passer and they have determined the ball's flight, height, and direction but they all approach and jump. If the set pass is to one of the outside spikers it will be high enough to allow for the approach.

6. On each play the set passer has the option of setting to either of the three spikers. Verbal calls from the set passer can sometimes be used to prevent confusion for the spikers.

7. In this formation the center spiker is often used merely as a decoy. But this option must be used judiciously or it becomes ineffective.

8. This formation has some weaknesses:
   a. One player carries the entire responsibility for set passing. She must be very capable.
   b. Only two players in the back court are left to cover against a block.

9. This offensive formation can be elected only if the abilities of the individual team members warrant it. It is not as "safe" as the 4 - 2 system.

The 6 - 0 System of Offense

This system of team play can be used only if all players are capable spikers and efficient ball handlers. One of the spikers comes from the back line each time to perform the set passing role.

1. This system of offense is possible only with a superior team.

2. It allows three spiker-blockers on the front line at all times. It also reduces the back row coverage to field balls which get past the block or those blocks which are deflected back into the spiker's court.

3. It offers many options on the offense but these are possible only if all team members are highly skilled.

4. The method for getting the set passer to the front row is the same as

in the 5 - 1 system of offense when the set passer is on the back line; however, *any one* of the back line players can serve as set passer.

5. This is the system of offense used most often now in international competition and is being adopted by the most efficient teams in United States national competition.

SUMMARY

1. The spike is a difficult skill that requires progressive learning. Some progressions could be repeated periodically even after the spiker has gone through them all and has participated in game situations. Repetition aids the spiker to gain insight into her weaknesses.

2. The coach should be guided by the ability of her players and should strive to develop their maximum potentiality.

3. The spiker must learn the arm and hand movements and the resultant body rotation and then be able to coordinate them with a running approach, a maximum jump, and hitting a moving object.

4. The spiker must understand the importance of the waiting position and know when to start her approach.

5. The position of the spiking arm in its backswing is crucial.

6. It is important that the spiker know the appropriate contact point on the ball and the position of the arm in its swing if she is to spike effectively.

7. Advanced power spiking involves a straight forward approach, a two-foot take off, and hitting from the side line.

8. Advanced spikers "play the block" to their advantage and are adept at spiking the first pass.

9. The set passer is a key player not only because the spiker's effectiveness depends upon her ability but because she is instrumental in gauging the defensive play of the opponents and determining which spiker will be utilized.

10. The set passer must know her "ideal" position in relationship to the net, the "ideal" and a practical position to which the ball is set, and be a very skilled ball handler.

11. Mastery of the forward and backward overhand pass is a *must* for all team members.

12. The offensive pass is sometimes more effective than a spike. A change of pace is often invaluable.

13. The "dink" or "soft spike" is included in the repertory of all advanced spikers.

14. A team must be able to serve effectively in order to make points. A very good serve can be an offensive weapon. Placement of the serve is also strategic.

15. Offensive formations—the basic one, the 4 - 2, the 5 - 1, the 6 - 0—are selected to use the abilities of a specific group of individuals to their maximum advantage. No system within itself will be successful without finely developed basic ball handling skills.
16. The offensive team must be aware of covering vital areas of the court instead of standing to admire the performance of its spiker.
17. *The best of strategy is of no consequence without the mastery of basic techniques—first things first!*

4

Defensive Techniques

The old cliché, "The best defense is a good offense," is certainly true. Powerful, well-placed spikes and effective deceptive maneuvers by the offensive team make it difficult for the defensive team to field the ball adequately or to launch an offense. If the competition is good it is inevitable, however, for any team also to have to defend itself against its opponents. If both teams have powerful spikers the better defensive team has the margin necessary to win the match.

Definite defensive techniques must be learned and practiced until they can be utilized consistently. Defensive formations must be built around the abilities of the individuals comprising the team.

TECHNIQUE ANALYSIS AND DRILLS

The Block

Use

The block is a technique employed by one or more players to impede the progress of a spiked ball by:

1. Making the ball bounce back over the net, or
2. Deflecting the ball upward and backward to a teammate who can pass the ball forward to be spiked.

Body Mechanics

1. Potential blockers should watch the ball closely to determine whether or not the set pass will make an effective spike possible.
2. If the set pass is good, the blocker approaches to within one and a half to two feet of the net and stands on both feet with all joints flexed ready to jump.
   a. If one blocker is utilized she should station herself in line with the ball so that it will strike both her hands.

b. If two or more blockers are utilized they should stand as close together as possible so that the ball will be directly between them.

c. If the particular spiker consistently hits to her right the blockers should move slightly to that side rather than attempt to cover equal distances on both sides of the ball.

d. The block is set (its position determined) by the LF spiker when the spike comes from the opposing RF and by the RF spiker when the spike comes from the opposing LF. The spiker so determined takes her place and the other member or members of the block then position themselves beside her, ready to jump.

3. *Watch the spiker.* As she executes her take-off, the blockers *jump straight upward* with maximum extension of all joints and an upward thrust of the arms. The eyes *then watch the ball.*

4. The arms and hands assume their blocking position:

a. The elbows and the arms extend upward and *forward* so that the hands are approximately one foot in front of the vertical plane of the nose;

b. The wrist is cocked so that the fingers point upward or slightly backward;

c. The forefingers are approximately five inches apart; the thumbs are beside the forefingers at an approximate 45-degree angle; the fingers are slightly spread and *tense.*

5. If the blocker desires to send the ball back over the net, the tense fingers point directly upward and maintain this rigidity at contact.

6. If the blocker desires to deflect the ball backward for a teammate to pass she points the extended tense fingers slightly backward and "gives" with the impact.

7. After contact with the ball the blocker returns to the floor, turns to watch the ball, and moves into position for the play.

8. In Chapter 3 it was pointed out that advanced power spikers "play the block" to their advantage. A skillful blocker(s) can nullify the effect of the spiker's "playing the block" as illustrated previously in Figure 13 by:

a. Moving the appropriate arm and hand forward and

b. Turning the wrist to allow the open hand to counteract the angle of the spike (see Figure 35).

9. The blocker MUST NOT *touch the net* or, if she reaches over the net, *touch the ball prior to the spiker's contact.*

Coaching Suggestions

1. All players should be aware that a blocking player or players leave a big space unprotected on the court.

2. If a spiker is not a powerful hitter it is to the advantage of the team for each player to *be in her defensive position to handle the ball with an overhand pass.*

3. Even powerful spikers need not be blocked unless they get a good set pass. Potential blockers moving into position should return to their defensive positions immediately if the set pass is poor (too far over the net, too far back in the court, or at an inappropriate angle for the spiker).

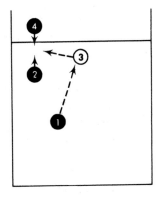

Figure 34

4. Blockers should jump straight upward rather than forward to avoid contacting the net.

5. The blocker should flex her ankles and knees upon landing to prevent shin splints and excessive internal jar.

Drills

1. Figure 34 shows a simple formation for beginner blockers having player #1 pass the ball to set passer #3, a spike by #2, and a block by #4.

   a. Rotate in some manner so that each player physically tall enough to block has an opportunity to do so.

   b. Three or four attempts should be made by each player before rotation.

2. Using the same drill, have two blockers instead of one. The ball will be directly between them.

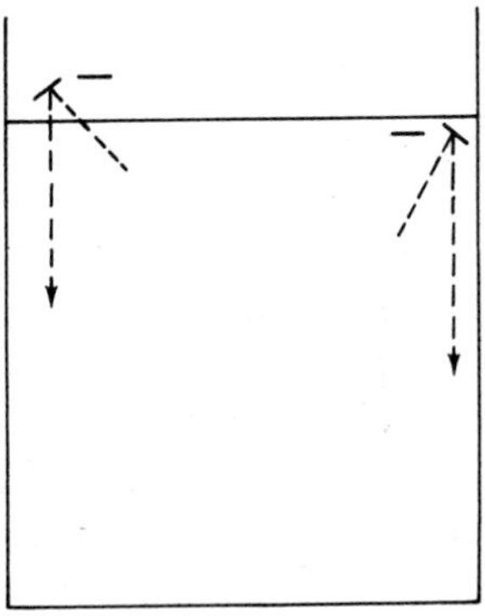

Figure 35

3. Figure 35 illustrates the counteraction of an angled spike by the block. The two short lines represent the hand positions of the blocker.

   a. On the left side of the court the spiker has hit the ball from right to left, depending upon the block to deflect it out of bounds. The right arm of the blocker moved forward with a turned wrist and hand to deflect the ball back over the net—in bounds.

   b. On the right side of the court the blocker has reached over the net, moved the left arm forward with a turned wrist, and deflects the angled spike back in bounds.

COMMON ERRORS

1. The blocker allows the spiker to hit over her hands by:
   a. Jumping too late, or
   b. Jumping too soon and dropping before the spike.

2. The blocker(s) reach over the vertical plane of the net.

3. The blocker closes her eyes and loses the ball.

4. The ball goes down the blockers' arms rather than rebounding across the net or being deflected backward.

5. The blocker extends her arms and hands directly overhead rather than forward, causing her to lose sight of the ball and allowing the spiker to hit around the block.

6. Players who are literally too short or those who are not consistently proficient jump at the net, supposedly to block.

COACHING HINTS

1. Watch the spiker—time the blocking take-off to correspond with hers; **then watch the ball.**

2. This is legal so long as the blocker(s) **do not touch the net** and **do not touch the ball before the spiker does.**

3. When the eyes have shifted from the spiker to the ball, keep them open and on the ball.

4. This can be **caused by:**
   a. Having the extended fingers in a straight line with the **forward** extension of the arms rather than cocking the wrist to allow fingers to extend straight upward or slightly backward, or
   b. The spiker's tapping rather than hitting the ball.
   A single blocker can do nothing in this eventuality because she has had one contact and cannot have another without an intervening hit. In cases of multiple blockers, however, one of them may contact the ball again following the block, even though only one of the jumping players actually contacted the ball. The player closest to this descending ball should drop a fist **immediately** and send the ball upward and backward for a teammate to hit across the net.

5. The hands should be approximately one foot in front of the vertical plane of the nose to enable the blocker to see the ball at all times and to follow its path with her blocking hands.

6. This should be discouraged generally, because the blocker leaves a "hole" in her defensive position. Occasionally, however, a jumping player on the opposite side of the net will disconcert the **inexperienced** spiker.

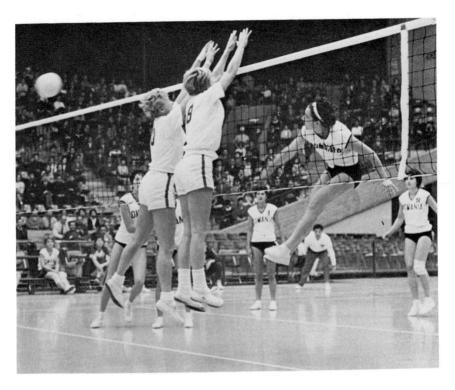

Tokyo, October 13, 1964. America's Nancy Owen (3) and Linda Murphy (8) block a Rumanian spiked ball. Rumania won the match (15 - 9, 15 - 1, 15 - 2).

This illustrates the ball rebounding from the block at a decided angle, probably out of bounds. (Courtesy of Compix)

Notice the position of the arms and hands of the blockers. They did not counteract the angled spike (the spiker has hit from left to right with a follow-through to her right side).

Fielding Spikes

In the game of power volleyball hard-driven spikes are common-place. The block is the best defense. Often, however, the blockers fail to contact the ball because the spiker hits over, around, or through them. Occasionally potential blockers miscalculate the ability of a spiker to hit a poor set pass and fail to block the subsequent spike. One of several techniques can be employed to field the spike, that is, receive the spike and get the ball to a teammate who can control the pass. These techniques include:

1. The forward overhand pass
2. An underhand hit with one fist (dig pass)
3. An underhand hit with the forearms (bump pass)
4. A one hand overhead pass

The forward overhand pass, which has already been discussed in detail in Chapter 3, is by all standards the most desirable technique to use in fielding a ball because it allows maximum control in passing. The rapid speed of a hard-driven spike often makes it impossible, however, for even the most skilled and agile player to get in a position to use this pass. Other techniques thus have to be learned, *though none is as desirable as the overhand pass* simply because no other technique allows the same degree of accuracy and control.

The other techniques listed for fielding a spike are explained in detail in Chapter 5, Auxiliary Skills.

DEFENSIVE FORMATIONS

Court Position for Receiving the Service

One of the most noticeable weaknesses in the teamwork or strategy of a novice team is the formation for receiving the service—the front line stands close to the net and the back line stands close to the end line, exposing the *vital area of the court* (that portion of the court where the majority of balls hit the floor). The fallacy of this formation is evident because:

1. The server does not serve so that the ball drops directly over the net.
2. The back line player standing just in front of the end line will be utilizing the overhand pass on balls that would be out. In all probability all balls that would be inside the court have to be handled with an underhand hit, which *greatly reduces accuracy and control* and which leads to the probability of *lifting or throwing* the ball.

Illustrations

(Numbers indicate serving order or position on the court.)
1. Figure 36 diagrams four spikers and two set passers with the set passer starting CF.
   a. Set passer #3 is close to the net;
   b. Spikers #2 and #4 are about 15 feet from the net;
   c. Spikers #1 and #5 are 8 to 10 feet in front of the end line;

d. Set passer #6 is about two feet in front of the other two backs;

e. The five players in the backcourt form a "W."

2. Figure 37 diagrams four spikers and two set passers with the set passer starting as the RF.

a. Player #2 will switch as soon as the ball is contacted on the service.

b. Should the service come to that area of the court occupied by spiker #3, she will field the service while set passer #2 is moving into her position to set.

3. Figure 38 shows four spikers and two set passers with the set passer starting as the LF.

a. Player #4 will switch as soon as the service is contacted.

b. Should the service be delivered to the CF position, spiker #6 will field the ball while set passer #4 is moving into the CF position to set.

4. If the 5 - 1 or 6 - 0 system of offense is used, refer to Figures 31-33 in Chapter 3 for placement of players on the service.

Coaching Suggestions

1. The set passer on the front row should always stand close to the net in the location from which she will set. She should not field the service because the service itself is generally difficult to set and the most advantageous position from which to make the set pass is close to the net —that distance from the net at which the set pass is placed; thus it is logical that a teammate field the ball and pass it to her.

2. Front line players, with the exception of the set passer, stand approximately 15

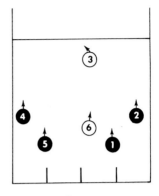

Figure 36

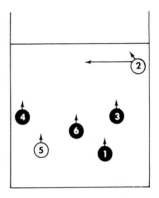

Figure 37

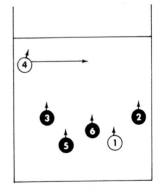

Figure 38

feet from the net. Back line players stand 8 to 10 feet in front of the end line.

3. See Figure 36 for the *imaginary division* of the court (five lines on the end line) for receiving the service. Attempt to have a player in each "lane"—which goes from the net to the end line so that each of the five receivers is responsible for a "lane" which is narrow and long. The set passer is excluded in these five positions because she should not receive the service.

4. This particular "lane" assignment necessitates the player's moving forward for short serves. If one knows the serving habits of the opponents, the initial receiving position may be altered; that is, the players can be positioned closer to the net to begin with for a server who consistently serves short serves.

5. If the team encounters a referee who will not allow them to receive the service with anything other than a bump, they may then wish to move their original positions farther back in the court.

6. It will be difficult to get a novice team to see the advantage of this formation. These players want to stand "under" the net and just in front of the end line. Back row players will feel at first as though they are "playing on the front row." The teacher or coach will have to be most *persistent* in encouraging this alignment and in demonstrating on every opportune play the disadvantage of any other formation.

7. This particular alignment is advantageous because:

   a. The overhand pass is the most desirable of all methods of fielding a ball—service or otherwise.

   b. A server does not place the ball a foot or two over the net—it is too difficult and inaccurate. Should the service be relatively short, however, it will not be travelling at a great speed and an alert player would certainly have time to take a step or several steps, bend the knees, and execute an overhand pass.

   c. If a service is a *hard-driven* one and is going to the back row, a player standing 10 feet or so inside the end line can handle it with an overhand pass. If this hard-driven service is too high for her to field, it will, in all probability, be out of bounds and she need not field it.

   d. If the service is high and out of reach of the back row player and is going to drop into the court behind her, it will of necessity be relatively slow because of its arc, and all she has to do is *move backward a few steps* to field the ball with an overhand pass.

8. Players must be reminded repeatedly to *watch the ball as it leaves the server's hand; determine its direction as quickly as possible;*

MOVE THE FEET and be in position to field the ball with an over-hand pass.

9. Fielding a service with an underhand hit indicates a poor alignment for the service or a failure of the player to MOVE or both.

10. In some cases referees force players to field services with a bump even though many leaders in the "volleyball movement" are trying to eliminate it. A SERVICE CAN BE RECEIVED LEGALLY WITH AN OVERHAND PASS.

11. Fielding the service with an underhand hit is definitely disadvantageous because it is so difficult to control, there is the danger of lifting or throwing, and this is time to assume the offensive role and win the service back before the opposing spiker has an opportunity to "kill the ball."

12. Players must be reminded constantly to "back up" teammates who are in the process of handling the ball. "Backing up" is discussed in this chapter under coverage of vital areas.

13. Since novice players are generally unaccustomed to this proper court alignment for service, they will take every available opportunity to let the teacher know that it did not work. THE BEST OF COURT ALIGNMENTS IS NOT EFFECTIVE 100 PERCENT OF THE TIME, but one must consider the odds. THE ODDS ARE IN FAVOR OF THIS ALIGNMENT. Generally a poor play is caused by the failure of players to watch the service, to determine its direction, and to MOVE. Occasionally a player will get caught with a particularly well-placed service, *but not as often* as with front row players standing "under the net" and back row players standing "on the end line."

Coverage of Vital Areas

One of the criticisms made by people who are not familiar with power volleyball is "Volleyball is not a very active game." This could not be farther from the truth. The more skilled the player the more active she is. THE SKILLED PLAYER MOVES ALL THE TIME THE BALL IS IN PLAY ON EITHER SIDE OF THE NET. She becomes a liability to the team when she becomes a "spectator on the court." Novice players ask, "But where do I go?" FOLLOW THE BALL. Players sometime become so obsessed with their particular court position that they fail to realize that *court position is determined in relation to the particular play in progress.*

The formations necessary for covering vital areas of the court when a teammate is in the process of spiking were discussed in Chapter 3. Formations for receiving the service were discussed previously in this chapter. These two fundamental areas of strategy are of paramount importance. In addition, this section will deal with strategy involved in:

1. Covering for blocking teammates.
2. Covering for teammates who are fielding the service, fielding a spike, or passing the ball in any other situation.

Covering for Blocking Teammates

Again the players must realize that court position is determined in relation to the play in progress. When one or more teammates move to the net to block, a space is left unprotected. The important thing to do at any moment is to position all players in the most advantageous position possible. Six players cannot physically occupy the entire court. A great difficulty in educating players is to teach them to assume one formation and then move immediately into another as the situation demands. On a block one of several things may happen:

a. The spiker may jump high enough to spike down behind the blockers, a situation which is very rare.
b. The spiker may hit directly into the block and have it rebound into the spiker's court.
c. The spiker may "play the block" or hit at such an angle that the spike rebounds from the blockers' hands—either into the blockers' court or out of bounds if the spiker is hitting from the side line.
d. The ball may go down the arms of the blockers because of their hand positions or because the spiker tapped the ball lightly.
e. The spiker may hit through the block.
f. The spiker may tip the ball over and behind the blockers.
g. The blockers may jump too soon or too late and have the spike tip against their finger tips but be ineffective in slowing the ball down.
h. The blockers may deflect the ball upward and backward for a teammate to pass to the spiking forward.

The problem, therefore, is to devise a formation or formations that can be as effective as possible for so wide a range of possibilities. For some of these there is no recourse.

a. If the block rebounds the ball to the spiker's court, the team will immediately begin to form a defense for a spike or another block.
b. If the block rebounds the ball out of bounds it is an automatic loss of point or service for the blocking team.
c. If the ball goes down the arms of a multiple block about the only possibility is a fist of one of the blockers dropped under the ball in order to bat it upward and backward.

But this still leaves several possibilities for the team to defend.

Illustrations

1. Figure 39 diagrams a spike by the opposing #8.
    a. #2 and #3 move to the net to block.
    b. Player #4 can use a dig pass should the ball be deflected to that side by the blockers.
    c. Player #5 or #1 can field a ball ineffectively blocked by or hit through the blockers.
    d. If the block deflects the ball upward and backward, #5 or #1 can set it for #4 to spike.
    e. Player #6 can field a ball tipped over and behind the blockers.

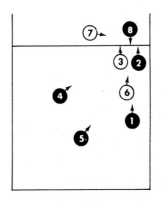

Figure 39

The cluster of players tends to be to the right side of the court because the majority of the time the spiker will hit straight forward or *slightly* to her right rather than sharply right because of the mechanical difficulty involved. Players #1, #4, and #5 should not be too far back in the court, because a hard-driven spike going through the block or barely touched by it can be handled with an overhand pass by those players. If the spike is hard driven and cannot be reached, it will probably be out of bounds. A ball deflected upward and backward will have been slowed down and have enough arc to enable #5 or #1 to move into position to pass.

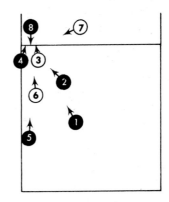

2. Figure 40 diagrams another possibility:
    a. If set passer #3 is tall enough, she blocks.
    b. The same possibilities are considered here as were stated in illustration #1 for Figure 39.

Figure 40

    c. The cluster is to the left side of the court because it would be almost impossible for spiker #8 to hit the ball sharply to her left without throwing it.
3. Figure 41 shows a single RF spiker blocking the opposing LF spiker. If two blockers were used, the CF set passer #3 would be added.

4. In figure 42 the RF spiker has moved over to block the opposing CF spiker. It is better to have her move over and leave the LF spiker in a position to spike, should the blocking team have an opportunity to assume the offense following a deflected ball on the block.

   Should two blockers be used, the #4 or LF spiker would assist #2.

5. It was pointed out in Chapter 3 that the offensive team should cover vital areas when its spiker hits. Figure 43 (p. 75) diagrams both the offensive and defensive teams.

   a. The A team's #3 is spiking.
   b. The B team's #3 and #4 are blocking.
   c. Note that each team assumes a formation simultaneously—an advantageous grouping for the particular play in progress.

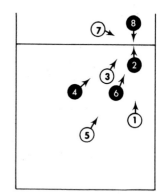

Figure 41

Coaching Suggestions

1. These diagrams presented relative to position on coverage of vital areas for defense purposes are suggestions which take into consideration the possibilities that may occur.

2. The coach should build her particular formations around the specific abilities of her individual players.

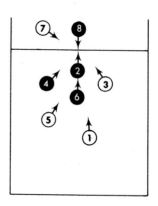

Figure 42

3. The team members should play together enough to know the strengths and weaknesses of the other players.

   a. Each player should become familiar with her specific defensive duties for each court position.
   b. These duties may change if a substitute replaces a regular starter because of the difference in abilities of the two players.

4. If the blockers decide not to block the defensive formation will change immediately.

5. It is most important that defensive players watch the body position of the opponent who is to hit the ball across the net. An alert player becomes aware of a spiker's body position while it is in the air on the jump to spike, and can usually predict the direction the spike will take,

though occasionally a spiker is so deceptive that she conceals it.

a. If a spiker uses a diagonal approach
and a one-foot take-off she will probably hit to her right more often than
straight away.

b. If she uses the straight approach and
two-foot take-off her range of hitting
will be broader, though most hits will
go right or straight forward because
this is easier mechanically, provided
she actually hits rather than pushes
the ball.

6. The important factor in defensive positioning is to determine the opponent's
offensive pattern as quickly as possible
and place players where the *majority* of
balls seem to be going.

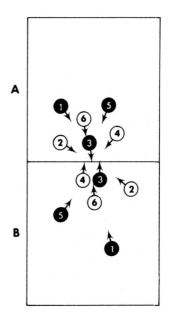

Figure 43

Covering for Teammates Who Are Fielding the Service, Fielding a Spike, or Passing the Ball in Any Other Situation

It was pointed out earlier that novice
players asking, "But where should I move?"
should be instructed to follow the ball. A
player should move toward or "back up" a
teammate in the process of handling the ball
in order to give assistance if needed. The
spiker and set passer will not move out of
position as far or as often as the other team
members.

Illustrations

1. Figure 44 shows a ball coming over the
net to be received by #5.

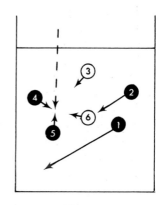

Figure 44

a. All players face the ball.

b. Player #1 runs rapidly to a position behind #5 to be there should
#5 tip the ball behind her accidentally instead of passing it
forward.

c. Player #2 moves several steps in that direction should either
player #5 or player #1 need her assistance because they are unable
to get the ball to its desired destination.

d. Players #6, #3, and #4 move a step or two in that direction to be of assistance if needed.

e. After #5 has contacted the ball, all players move in the direction of the new ball handler.

2. Figure 45 shows a ball coming over the net to player #2 and the movement of the team members to "back her up."

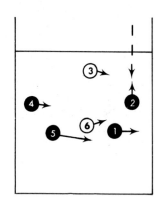

Figure 45

Drill

A player on the opposite side of the net will throw or serve a ball. All other team members will move to their respective positions.

a. When this drill or technique is first presented to a group of players, the receiver should catch the ball and all other team members stop their movement at that moment so that they can see their court position. The teacher can then point out the weaknesses in their movement patterns.

b. As proficiency in movement is attained, the ball can be played over the net while determining the team's ability to assume the offensive role.

Coaching Suggestions

1. A generalization of "backing up" assignments is: every player *watches and moves toward the ball* with the distance to be moved determined by court position.
   a. The CB backs up the entire front row.
   b. The outside backs (left and right) back up each other, the CB, and the front row.

2. A player should walk, slide, or run to her position, depending upon the distance to be covered. She should see the ball at all times.

3. A player can get too close to be of assistance to the person she is backing up. Her objective is to handle the ball if the receiver makes an error and deflects the ball rather than passes it to the intended receiver.

SUMMARY

1. Defensive patterns must be built around the abilities of the individual members and practiced until they are consistently effective.

2. The block is an essential defensive technique in power volleyball.

Notice the follow-through position of the spiker's arm with the turned wrist. She is left handed hitting from the left side of her own court. She has angled the hit to rebound off the block out-of-bounds. Notice also the position of the arms of the blocker on the right side of the picture. Her left arm is forward; this would counteract a spike should it have been hit from left to right by the spiker.

Tokyo, October 23, 1964. Japan's #8 spikes against the USSR (Courtesy of Compix)

3. A team may utilize a single blocker or a multiple block consisting of two or three players. The number is determined by the skill of the opposing spiker.

4. Balls which come over the net and are not blocked must be fielded in some manner, the most desirable being the overhand pass.

5. One of the most strategic defensive formations is that for receiving the service. This is the team's opportunity to prevent the opponents from scoring and to assume the offensive role.

6. The formation for receiving the service should be determined by considering the odds in service placement.

7. The remaining players must position themselves to cover vital court areas when a teammate or teammates are blocking because they leave spaces in the court.

8. Blocking assignments are determined by abilities of individual team members and may be dictated somewhat by the set of rules employed.

9. Various court positions have "backing up" assignments. Proficiency of team members in assuming these assignments often makes the difference in "saving the ball" or losing a point or the service.

10. The key to good defensive play is constant MOVEMENT.

chapter 5

Auxiliary Skills

The skills discussed in this chapter have been termed auxiliary ones because they are used both offensively and defensively. It is difficult to classify them exclusively under either of those two headings.

TECHNIQUE ANALYSIS AND DRILLS

Underhand Hitting

Underhand hitting is not desirable because these hits cannot be controlled very well and there is a strong possibility of lifting or throwing the ball. Skilled players use underhand hitting less often than novices because they are more conscious of the necessity to move and are more adept at doing so; they learn to anticipate ball direction and have a better understanding of offensive and defensive formations. But even the most skilled players occasionally find themselves in a situation where the underhand hit must be employed; therefore effective techniques must be developed. Players must realize that *these techniques are not as desirable as the overhand pass. They should be used only when the overhand pass is impossible,* even if the overhand pass must be executed in a full squat position (buttocks touching the heels and knees separated) or standing on kneepads.

Occasions for Use

1. When the ball is spiked directly at the receiver waist high or lower.
2. When the ball is spiked in a player's court area but she must reach for it, to either side or in front.
3. When a teammate passes the ball poorly so that it reaches the vicinity of the receiver waist level or lower.
4. When a player is moving away from the court to save a ball and has difficulty reaching it.
5. When a ball comes over the net from a block, a dink, or an offensive

pass and the receiver does not get there in time to position herself for an overhand pass.

Body Mechanics

1. The dig pass
   a. Contact may be made with either hand.
   b. The fist (either one) is made by clenching all knuckles of the fingers so that the nails are hidden and the thumb lies beside the forefinger.
   c. Contact is made with the whole flat surface of the fist—the heel of the hand and the flat second knuckle of all fingers.
   d. The wrist is bent toward the lower arm so that there is a "shelf" formed by the fist.
   e. The elbow is bent. Its proximity to the body is determined by the distance between the body and the ball.
   f. The knees are definitely bent.
   g. The position of the feet and legs vary from a comfortable side stride position or a comfortable forward stride position to a full lunge on one foot either to the side or forward, depending upon the distance to be covered and the amount of time available to move.
   h. The more advanced players execute dives or the "Japanese roll" with the dig to save balls.
   i. The *primary leverage* is the flexing of the *elbow;* slight leverage may be applied from the shoulder together with the elbow leverage, particularly on hits that occur away from the body when the arm is almost fully extended.
   j. As contact with the ball is made the hand follows through *slightly* and stops abruptly.
   k. The ball must be *batted,* that is, leave the hand immediately, or a lifting foul occurs.
   l. The knees maintain their flexed or bent position until the ball is on its way. They supply no leverage on the hit.
   m. Direction of the hit is determined by the position of the forearm and hand at contact:
      (1) If an upward hit (for a teammate to pass or spike) is desired, the forearm and hand is parallel to the floor at contact and the hit is made primarily upward.
      (2) If a forward hit is desired (the player is facing the net and wants to hit from well back court to the forecourt or all the way across the net) the forearm and hand point forward and

downward toward the floor and the hit is made forward and upward rather than just upward.

(3) If a backward hit is desired (the player has her back to the net) she must definitely be under the ball with the forearm and hand pointing upward and forward away from her body; contact is made with an upward and backward hit which brings her forearm closer to her face.

2. The "bump" or forearm pass

   a. The position of the hands and forearms is established:

      (1) Lay the back of the fingers of one open hand across the inside of the fingers of the other open hand so that the two hands form a 90-degree angle;

      (2) Then fold the hands together so that the heels of the hands touch;

      (3) Extend the two thumbs forward side by side so that they lie across the forefinger of the top hand;

      (4) Rotate the elbows inward so that the entire forearms are close together. This position feels uncomfortable until one becomes accustomed to it, but it is functional. It offers a broad surface with which to contact the ball.

   b. Contact is made with the FOREARMS, just above the wrist.

   c. Leverage is primarily from the *shoulders.*

   d. The knees are DEFINITELY BENT with the feet and legs in a forward stride or side stride position.

   e. As contact with the ball is made:

      (1) The arms move forward and upward from the shoulder;

      (2) The knees begin to straighten.

   f. The arms follow through to a position about parallel to the floor.

   g. The legs follow through to a straight knee position.

   h. Direction of the ball's flight is determined by the position of the arms at contact with the ball in their swing forward and upward (with a position in which they are pointing downward as 6:00). Using a clock face analogy, a contact with the ball at 9:00 in the *arm swing* (a position in which they are parallel to the floor) would send the ball *directly upward;* a contact at 8:00 in the arm swing would send the ball *forward* as well as upward.

Drills

1. The drill in Figure 46 (p. 82) can utilize many players in practicing the dig and bump.

a. The teacher or coach decides which technique (*bump* or *dig*) is to be practiced at a particular time.

b. Player #4 *throws* the ball toward player #1 so that it reaches her *between waist and knee height,* either directly toward her or to either side (depending upon which technique is being practiced).

c. Player #1 executes the appropriate technique and has two options (which may also be directed by the coach):

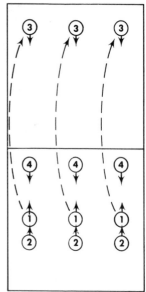

(1) She may send the ball all the way to the back court of the opponents;

(2) She may send the ball to #4 (who might represent *either* a set passer or a spiker).

d. Player #3 retrieves the ball and rolls or bounces it back under the net to #4.

e. Player #4 can throw the ball directly at #1 or slightly to the right or left. As proficiency is gained, she should be required to move rather than receive the ball within easy reach.

f. To rotate, #4 moves across the net, #3 moves behind #2, and #1 moves to the net to throw the ball.

Figure 46

g. In a game situation, bumping or digging the ball to the opponents' back court would be called for when the player is the third one to play the ball and it must be hit over the net.

2. This same formation in Figure 46 can be used to practice the backward dig pass.

a. Player #1 throws the ball to player #4 so that it reaches her between waist and knee level.

b. Player #4 executes a dig pass backward.

c. This pass is often necessary in a game because of a poor pass from the back row. The player at the net feels that she will be unable to set it with the dig pass and so "saves" the ball by sending it to the opposing back court.

3. Figure 47 diagrams players practicing the dig or bump pass with the side to the net.

a. Player #2 throws the ball to #1 so that it reaches her between waist and knee level;

b. Player #1 executes a dig or bump in order to send the ball to the opposite back court.

c. Or she may bump or dig as a *set pass* for #2 to spike.

d. The coach designates the type of pass to be used.

4. The same type of formation (Figure 47) can be used by having the throwing line shift in the opposite direction so that the dig or bump passer has her right side to the net.

5. Figure 48 diagrams another situation for using the backward underhand hit.

a. Player #4·throws the ball high and away from the receiver so that the latter must turn her back to the net and *run* in order to reach the ball.

b. The time consumed by the run does not allow #1 to run beyond the ball, turn to face the net, and execute an overhand pass;

c. She therefore reaches the ball with her back to the net and executes an *underhand hit* even though *the ball may be above her head.*

d. She hits the ball with a dig all the way to the opposite back court.

e. This may occur often in a game as a result of:

    1. A deflected hit by the block which sends the ball out of reach of a back court player;

    2. A well-placed offensive pass by the opponents which catches the receiver out of position;

    3. A long deflected hit by a teammate which causes the player responsible for backing her up to run a considerable distance to reach the ball.

6. Figure 49 diagrams a formation utilizing

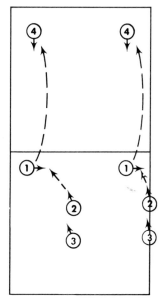

Figure 47

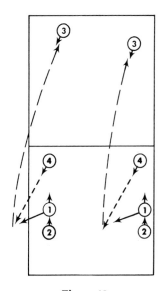

Figure 48

the dig or bump in order to set the ball for a spiker:

a. Player #2 throws the ball so that it reaches #1 between waist and knee level;
b. Player #1 sets the ball with a dig or bump;
c. Player #5 approaches the net and spikes;
d. Player #4 retrieves the ball and rolls it under the net to #2.

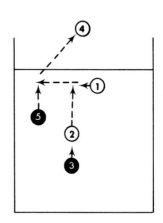

Figure 49

Coaching Suggestions

1. Underhand hitting should be used as a last resort. If it is possible for the receiver to move, to utilize a full squat position, or to stand on kneepads to execute an overhand pass she should do so.
2. Exceptions occur to the above rule when the moving distance required is too great or a long distance hit (third hit must travel across the net) is required.
3. Underhand hitting with an open hand is absolutely prohibited at national level competition in USVBA.
4. A player can reach farther with one hand than with two; consequently, if she has to do extensive reaching the dig should be utilized; otherwise the ball rolls off the fingers ineffectively.
5. The leverage for hitting underhand with *one fist* comes primarily from the *flexion of the elbow.*
6. If a ball is close to the receiver the broader hitting surface of the bump or forearm pass offers more control than the dig.
7. The leverage for the bump pass comes *primarily from the upward movement at the shoulder.*
8. It is most important that the knees be bent to allow the receiver to get *under the ball.*
9. If the dig pass is to go backward, the passer must get her fist under the ball far enough to be able to hit under the ball on that part of the ball farthest away from her so she can hit upward and backward.

One Hand Overhead for Distance

Occasions for Use

1. A well-placed offensive pass catches a player out of position; she must back up rapidly and does not have time to get behind the ball, in which position she could execute an overhand pass.

2. A player backing up a teammate does not have time to move behind the ball to pass overhand.
3. A player will use this technique on any other occasion in which she is facing the net and must contact the ball directly above her head. Mechanically, a player cannot reach *directly* above her head to contact the ball and use the overhand pass *forward* without throwing the ball.
4. A player with a weak pass caught well back in the court with the third hit for the team can use this technique to advantage in getting the ball to the opposing back court.

Body Mechanics

Refer to the section in Chapter 3 on body mechanics for the overhead service. The technique is the same with the following exceptions:
1. The player does not toss the ball but positions herself in a desirable relationship to it.
2. *Preferably the feet maintain contact with the floor,* but if the height of the ball demands it the player will jump into the air from both feet.

Drill

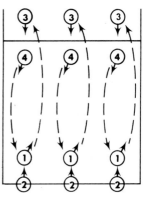

1. Figure 50 diagrams a drill for practicing the one-hand overhead hit for distance.
   a. Player #4 throws the ball so that it reaches the vicinity of #1 about arm's length above her head;
   b. Player #1 backs up a step or two and executes the overhead hit, attempting to send it over the net to the back court.
   c. As proficiency is gained the receiver should be forced to move backward

Figure 50

or to either side to reach the ball. *If she should have to travel forward the overhand pass is in order* (offensive pass).
2. The coach might also use a formation having the hitter send the ball to the set passer on the front row. If this is the first hit for a team, the most desirable placement for the overhead hit would be to the set passer so that the team could assume the offensive role.

Coaching Suggestions

1. The hit should be made with an *open hand* and not a fist. The player has just as much power with the heel of the hand and the fingers aid in giving control and direction.
2. If a player has to move forward in order to use this technique, she

could probably pass overhand to better advantage unless she has great difficulty getting distance with the overhand pass. This technique does not provide as much accuracy.

3. The player should keep her eyes on the ball.
4. Stress those occasions in which this technique *should* be used.
5. This is the same hit described as "spike type" hitting in Chapter 3.

One-Fist Overhead as a "Save" (a "Punch")

Occasion for Use

If a ball from the back row reaches the front row *too high* to be handled with an overhand pass it should be "punched" over the net. This might result because:

a. The ball is travelling fast on a plane parallel to the floor but is not quite clear of the net; the set passer cannot reach this high to set a fast moving ball adequately.
b. The ball is travelling on a high arc and reaches the net too high for the set passer to receive without committing a net foul, but the ball would drop down the net without going over.

Body Mechanics

1. The receiver is facing away from the net watching the ball and determines that the one-fist overhead will have to be used. She maintains this posture facing away from the net and watches the ball with all joints slightly flexed.
2. One fist is clenched as for a dig pass.
3. As the ball gets directly overhead she springs *straight upward* from both feet and "punches" the ball.
   a. The elbow which was flexed slightly prior to the jump is fully extended, the biceps are close to the ear, and the wrist is straight;
   b. The ball is contacted with the flat top of the fist (that part with which a boxer would hit his opponent);
   c. The fist contacts the ball on its extreme *bottom*.
4. The body and extended arm follow through straight upward.
5. The player returns to the floor at the spot from which she jumped.
6. She *then turns* to watch the flight of the ball.

Drill

Figure 51 shows a drill for practicing the one fist overhead "save":

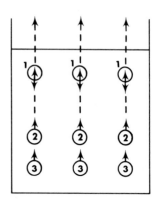

Figure 51

1. Player #2 throws the ball so that it definitely necessitates the one-fist overhead (see occasion for use).
2. Player #1 executes the one-fist overhead hit, preferably to the back court.
3. The retriever across the net rolls the ball back.
4. Rotation puts #2 at the net, #1 to retrieve, and the retriever moves behind #3.

Coaching Suggestions

1. The situations in which this technique should be used happen often in games. Players should practice the technique frequently enough to be able to use it "instinctively."
2. This is definitely a "save" play because the opposition can field it easily, but the action is better than having the ball die at the net.
3. The player using this technique *should not turn as she contacts the ball.*
4. She should "punch" straight upward and follow through upward, *not toward the net.* This latter practice will probably result in a net foul. *The ball has enough speed to get over the net; it simply needs height.*
5. If the ball travelling with an arc drops low enough and soon enough, the front row player should set the ball if she is making the second hit, or pass offensively if she is making the third hit.

Use of Kneepads

Occasions for Use

1. A player falls onto and slides on the kneepads in order to field a ball with an overhand pass or dig pass when she would not have time to field it by squatting.
2. The kneepads offer protection if a player loses her balance and falls while moving for a ball. (Note that the international players in the photographs use knee pads.)

Body Mechanics

1. The player flexes the knees.
2. She pushes off forcefully with one foot as though she were beginning a track sprint from a standing position.
3. As the opposite leg starts forward it bends sharply so that the body will land on the knee and lower leg, with the toes extended behind the body.
4. After the push, the take-off foot bends at the knee and moves forward to slide parallel with the other knee.
5. The player then executes the overhand pass, dig, or bump.

Drill

Two or three players stand facing the same direction with another player 12 to 15 feet in front of them.

1. The front player throws the ball with a slight arc (the highest part of the arc about six feet) so that the ball will strike the floor about two feet in front of the receiver.
2. Just after the ball leaves the thrower's hand the receiver pushes off and slides onto her knees, covering as much distance as possible with the push and slide.
3. She executes an overhand pass if possible, if not, a dig or bump. She attempts to pass the ball so that the thrower can receive it and execute an overhand pass.

Footwork

The volleyball teacher or coach constantly tells players to "MOVE!" This necessitates some kind of footwork. The type and amount of moving required is determined by the court position and the caliber of competition. It would be impossible to give a detailed analysis of all the movement possibilities, so some generalizations follow.

1. Specific suggestions for movement patterns involved in covering vital areas of the court for spiking, blocking, and backing up teammates were given in Chapter 3 and Chapter 4.
2. Specific suggestions for the spiker's approach to the net were made in Chapter 3.
3. The set passer faces the back court (generally) to watch the original ball receiver.
   a. She may have to step forward or backward to align herself with the descending ball;
   b. Then as it approaches she turns with a pivot or successive short sideward steps in order to get her side to the net while she watches the ball over her shoulder.
4. Players utilize forward and backward walking and running steps and slides to the side, always attempting to keep their eyes on the ball.
   a. A player may take one step forward, then two straight backward;
   b. She might run forward three steps and slide once right;
   c. She might run forward two steps and slide onto her kneepads.
5. There is no definite and set number or kind of movement; all movement is relative to the flight of the ball.
6. Players follow the movement of the ball while it is in play on both sides of the net.
7. Players watch the ball at all times. As soon as it leaves the hitter's

hands they try to determine its direction and rate of speed, and move to a position to receive it or to carry out assignments in terms of reinforcing a teammate.

Drills

1. Specific movement drills have been given for practicing certain techniques in this and the two previous chapters.
2. A simple drill to practice movement together with various ball handling techniques is presented in Figure 52.
   a. The center player #6 passes the ball to the same vicinity each time;
   b. Player #1 passes the ball back to her, then moves on around the circle in a counterclockwise direction;
   c. Player #2 then approaches the area to which #6 will pass the ball;
   d. Each player knows when it is her turn to receive the ball;
   e. She should attempt to get her pass to #6 so that #6 has no difficulty receiving it with an overhand pass (medium high arc dropping about a foot in front of her nose);

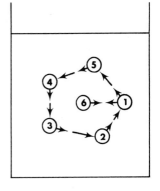

Figure 52

   f. The player runs forward until she nears the hitting area (always with her eyes on the ball as she looks over her shoulder);
   g. Then she turns her body to face #6 and uses sliding steps sideward;
   h. From this slide she may have to take forward or backward slow or quick steps in order to align herself with the ball;
   i. After she has made the pass she takes another slide or two to watch the ball and then takes forward walking or running steps;
   j. To acquaint novice players with various movement the coach might have all players in this circle formation with no ball, and verbally call commands for them to follow and count or beat a dance drum to accent the speed of the step and change the pace often. For example: side -2 -3; forward -2 -3 -4; slide -2; back -2 -3 (and of these four movement patterns three might be fast and one slow);
   k. The center player #6 in the drill could be an experienced player and vary the hits required by the receivers: easy overhand pass, overhand pass in a squat position, dig pass close to the receiver,

dig pass to either side of the receiver, kneepad hit, one-hand over-head hit, etc.

l. The coach should make suggestions all the time the drill is going on, pointing out improvements that could be made in the technique used or an alternative technique that would have been more appropriate. She can make individual comments to a player as she moves from the hitting vicinity on around the circle.

Recovering the Ball from the Net

This is a most difficult technique. When a ball enters the net travelling fast and parallel to the floor, most nets will rebound the ball relatively parallel to the floor and a player simply has to use a dig or bump to get it either to a teammate or over the net. But this is not what happens 99 per cent of the time. Generally the ball is passed toward the net in an arc and falls down the net rather than rebounding from it.

Occasion for Use

The ball enters the net because:

1. A pass intended for a receiver on the front row is too long and the ball falls into the net.
2. A player attempts to pass the ball across the net but it drops short and falls down the net.

Body Mechanics

1. A front row player watching a pass determines that it is going into the net and sees that she is unable to execute the one fist overhead "save" technique.
2. She immediately drops into a deep squat position.
   a. The side of the body should be toward the net;
   b. The foot closer to the center line should be very close to the line;
   c. The feet may be in a forward or side stride position;
   d. The knees are flexed to a maximum;
   e. The eyes never leave the ball.
3. The player executes a dig pass to send the ball upward and backward to a teammate.
   a. The ball is contacted just before it reaches the floor;
   b. A dig pass with one fist gives the passer more freedom of movement on this hit.

Drill

Figure 53 diagrams a drill for practicing the recovery of a ball from the net:

1. Player #3 throws the ball in an arc so that it hits the net and drops down it.
2. Player #1 recovers the ball.
3. If possible, #2 spikes; if not, the player receiving the ball from the recovery passes offensively to send the ball over the net.
4. Player #1 should not assume the squat position before the ball hits the net; she should practice the drop into position as the ball hits the net.

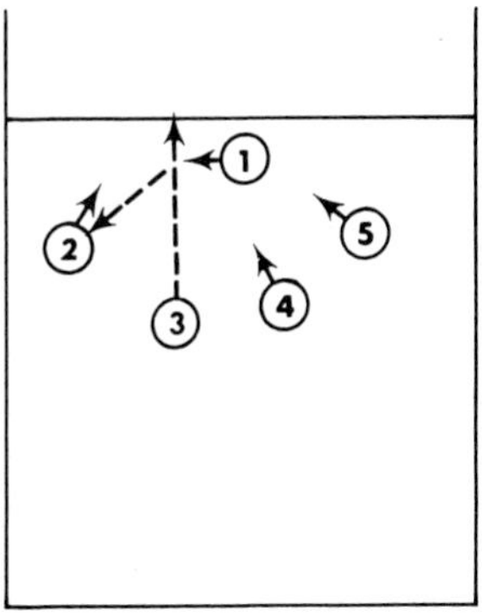

Coaching Suggestions

1. Recovering the ball from the net is very difficult and not very accurate; if at all possible the player should jump to use the fist overhead in order to keep the ball from going into the net.
2. It is most important that the player drop into a deep squat immediately if a recovery is necessary.
3. The player should have her *side to the net* rather than the front of her body.
4. She should be there waiting for the ball as it drops out of the net and wait until the last possible moment to contact the ball; this gives her longer to time her movement in relation to the ball's movement.
5. The dig pass gives more movement range for the passer; the leverage for this hit comes primarily from the elbow.
6. If this player is making the third hit for the team she must attempt to hit it over the net, but it is almost impossible if the ball is dropping straight down the net; otherwise she attempts to pass the ball upward and backward for a teammate to pass or spike.

Figure 53

Verbal Signals

Occasions for Use

1. Blockers at the net indicate whether or not they contact the ball as it comes over. This is done for the benefit of the referee and teammates.
2. A player indicates whether or not she will receive a ball if there is any doubt as to which of two players should do so.
3. An experienced player who is a good team player and is familiar with formations and abilities of the various team members may call plays.
4. The CF set passer may indicate which forward should spike.

Techniques

1. A blocker or blockers yell "NO!" if they do not contact the spiked ball on *their* side of the net (the spiked ball went into and not over the net).
   a. If the spiked ball hits them *through the net* then there can be no recovery by the teammates of the spiker;
   b. If the "NO" signal is given and the spiked ball goes out of bounds, side out or point is awarded to the blocking team.
   c. If the "NO" signal is given and the spiked ball enters the blockers' court, teammates then know that they may have three contacts.
2. A blocker or blockers yell "ONE!" if they contact the spiked ball.
   a. If the block deflects the ball out of bounds teammates know they must attempt to recover the ball.
   b. Teammates also know that they have only two hits remaining.
3. Often a ball could be fielded by either of two players. A verbal signal such as "MINE," "I'VE GOT IT," "YOURS," or "TAKE IT" will eliminate such possibilities as:
   a. Each player thinking the other is going to get the ball and thus both stand and watch it hit the floor;
   b. Both players moving to field the ball and interfering so that the pass is unsuccessful;
   c. Both players moving to field the ball and colliding. This could result in an injury.
4. Often a team will have a player who is exceptionally good at perceiving advantageous formation and the hesitancy of players to move into position. If she has the type of personality which allows her to do so without creating enmity she can call names of players who are to play the ball, indicate blocking assignments, give hints to the set passer relative to the opponents' defense patterns, etc. This is done constantly as the game progresses.
5. At times the CF set passer sets the ball so that there is doubt as to which player will spike the ball. The set passer should call one spiker's name to avoid:
   a. A delayed start by the spiker which prohibits a spike and necessitates a pass;
   b. The spiker watching the ball runs into the set passer, who moved expecting the other spiker to hit.
6. The CF set passer can indicate verbally which spiker should get ready for the set. If the opponents are familiar with the names of the players, some signal other than the spiker's name will have to be used or the blockers will be forewarned.

7. A player should call "OUT!" if a teammate gets ready to field a ball coming from the opponents' court; the player calling the signal may be in a more advantageous position to judge the speed and direction of the ball.

Coaching Suggestions

1. Players should be encouraged to use verbal signals.
2. They should all be familiar with appropriate signals.
3. Talking and yelling help to release tension.
4. Verbal commendation for good plays of teammates should be encouraged.
5. Teammates who tend to become depressed or discouraged should be encouraged verbally.

SUMMARY

1. Auxiliary skills are used by a team on both defense and offense.
2. Underhand hitting is not as desirable as the overhand pass because of the lack of control and the danger of a lifting foul.
3. Even the most skilled and agile player must use the underhand hit occasionally.
4. The underhand hit may be a dig or a bump.
5. A hit with one-hand overhead is used advantageously in several game situations where the overhand pass is impossible or inadvisable.
6. A "punch" with one fist overhead often prevents having to recover the ball from the net; it provides a "save" technique to keep the ball in play, thus allowing the possibility of recovering the offensive role.
7. Kneepads afford players many opportunities to execute the overhand pass in preference to a dig pass; they also offer protection in falls.
8. Effective footwork is necessary in power volleyball; it can be analyzed, practiced, and developed.
9. Appropriate techniques should be used to prevent a ball from entering the net; it is almost impossible to recover the ball with the third hit; a ball hitting the net from the first contact can be recovered with efficient movement and a dig pass.
10. Teamwork can be strengthened by using appropriate verbal signals; talking can relieve excess tension and bolster a team's morale.

chapter 6

Warm-Up Drills

Players should warm up prior to strenuous physical activity for one basic reason—prevention of injury. Physiologically, warming up is desirable. When an individual engages in strenuous activity she breathes faster and her heart beats faster and with more force in order to provide the brain and muscles with the extra oxygen and nourishment necessitated by the workload. Mild activity—gradually intensified—aids in preventing strained or ruptured muscles which result from maximum muscular contraction. It prevents the strain which results from sudden increased demand. Cardiac, respiratory, and muscular endurance must be developed systematically over a period of time and the functions of these systems must be protected by intelligent use.

A secondary but very important contribution of warming up comes from the psychological preparation it provides. Psychological preparedness for the activity to be engaged in contributes immeasurably to success. Warming up should whet the appetite for stimulating and enthusiastic participation.

Warm-up drills and technique practice drills can also involve some of the specific elements of the game itself; consequently these drills aid not only as physiological "sets" but also in the development of the skill required for good play. Warm-ups can therefore contribute in this third way. Some warm-ups, however, are more general than specific.

WARM-UPS

Running

The practice of running two or three slow laps around the gymnasium or the playing court is excellent for the gradual increase of heart rate and for relieving the inevitable tension produced by competition.

Partner Passing

Each player passes overhand with a partner approximately five feet in front of her. This gives maximum participation in a short period of time.

Circle Passing

Each group is composed of five or six players who form a circle with one in the center. The center player passes the ball to the same location as the other players move in a clockwise direction with forward running and sideward sliding steps. The center player should be changed at frequent intervals.

Shuttle Passing

Each group is composed of five or six players who pass in a shuttle formation. Each player moves to her right after passing the ball, going to the end of the opposite line; moving in this specified direction allows players to avoid contact in passing. The two players at the head of each line should be approximately five feet apart.

Wall Spiking and Set Passing

The spikers have several balls and spike against the wall as described in Figure 4 while the set passers practice at the net as described in Figure 17.

Spiking and Set Passing

The team executes the drill described in Figure 10. Each spiker and set passer practices with her regular partner. One set passer may set the ball for two consecutive spikers or one spiker may spike balls from two consecutive set passers if this will be the situation in a game situation.

Serving

Half of the players stand behind each service line on the court and serve balls back and forth across the net.

Several specific activities have been designated above as warm-up drills. The coach can also select any skill drills included in the technique sections of this book or design other activities for warming up.

SUMMARY

1. Players should warm up prior to strenuous physical activity to prevent injuries and to condition the body physiologically.
2. Players should warm up prior to strenuous physical activity, especially a competitive event, to condition themselves psychologically.
3. Specific drills included in this chapter involve running, partner passing, circle passing, shuttle passing, wall spiking, set passing, spiking and set passing, and serving.
4. The coach can also select any skill drill, combine drills, or devise her own.

chapter 7

Modified Games

Volleyball is fun! Wherever large groups of people congregate for recreation one can usually find some persons playing volleyball because it can be played in almost any locality and the equipment is inexpensive and generally available.

Many potential enthusiasts are discouraged by rules and regulations. The highly-skilled performer finds rules and regulations helpful in her game and an asset in the orderly conduct of competition, but the unskilled and novice player is hampered and often discouraged. If the unskilled or novice player learns that volleyball can be fun and that advanced skills are even more fun, she will want to play more and practice those techniques which are used by the power volleyball player.

One way to nurture the interest and enthusiasm of the unskilled and novice player is to modify the rules and regulations so that she can have fun and at the same time improve her skills. Eventually she may develop enough skill to feel that regulation rules, rigidly enforced, offer a framework for the most stimulating game.

The teacher or coach can devise her own modified games. She can make up and add or delete rules according to the skill of her group. The important factors are:

1. Players should have fun.
2. Players should be introduced to good fundamental techniques so that they have a firm foundation on which to build skill.
3. Players should experience some degree of success, even if rules have to be simplified.
4. Players should be aware that there are more advanced techniques to be learned.
5. Players should be challenged to enter into the activity enthusiastically.

If the teacher will keep in mind that people like to play, that they like to achieve, that they are always challenged by new learning experiences that do not create embarrassment—if she can use her imagination to create new and interesting ideas and situations that do not threaten the individuals in the group, then she will have no difficulty maintaining enthusiasm and will find that girls *want to learn* the techniques which will further enhance their enjoyment.

It is important that leaders, teachers, and coaches be aware that rules are relative—their purpose is to provide a framework in which to function *effectively*. Several modified game situations are presented in this chapter. They are arranged in order from the simplest up to that which most nearly approximates a regulation game. It is emphasized that they are "modified"—and that they *can be further modified* to fit a particular situation. They can be changed as the situation changes. The group using such modifications, however, should be aware that it is not experiencing the official rules of the game.

SPECIFIC GAMES

Mass Volleyball

This game can be played by any number of players per team. Figure 54 shows 12—an arbitrary number. The following rules prevail:

a. The ball is "served" by a player who stands behind the end line and *throws* the ball over the net.

b. A team must serve in order to win a point.

c. If the receiving team commits an error the serving team scores.

d. If the serving team commits an error the receiving team wins the serve—side out.

e. A team rotates when it receives the service.

f. Rotation is in the form of a "backward S" (Figure 54 numbers the players in their serving order).

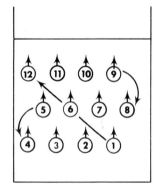

Figure 54

g. Errors

   1. A team allows the ball to hit the floor within its court (balls landing on the boundary line are good).

   2. A team propels the ball out of bounds and it hits the floor.

3. A player touches the net.

4. A player hits the ball before it crosses the net.

5. A player steps across the center line.

Suggestions for changes in the rules for mass volleyball follow. The teacher can implement these or other changes whenever she feels they are warranted.

a. The ball is *served* instead of thrown across the net.

b. Obvious holding, lifting, and throwing movements are called errors.

c. The holding, lifting, and throwing errors are more rigidly enforced (a ball must be *batted*—it must leave the hand immediately upon contact).

d. A maximum of five hits are allowed for each team.

e. A maximum of three hits is allowed for each team.

Stimulation Techniques

These are not modified games but are techniques to build interest and enthusiasm. A teacher may find that it is necessary to stimulate the group to work as a unit or practice "teamwork." An *esprit de corps* may be lacking. One of several techniques can be employed to remedy this difficulty:

a. The teacher calls time out and has each team form a huddle. In the huddle each girl is to find out the name of any girl she does not know. When play resumes after the huddle each girl is to congratulate the teammate who made a good play by name—at the time the good play occurs.

b. If a team loses two points consecutively its members must take a lap around the gymnasium. (This figure may be advanced to three or four points, depending upon the skill of the group.)

c. The teacher calls time out. Each team is to form a huddle and discuss possibilities for improving its performance.

1. Modified Game

This particular game #1 emphasizes the fact that the ball should be sent over the net by the spiker. Any number of players may be utilized. Figure 55 shows nine players numbered in their serving order; the solid

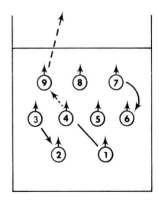

Figure 55

lines indicate movement of players in rotation for service; the dotted line indicates the ball crossing the net. Suggested rules are:

a. The service alternates. Each team serves every other ball.
b. A team scores a point each time the LF player (player #9 in Figure 55) sends the ball across the net into the court without committing a foul *(there is the possibility of making several scores with each service).*
c. Any number of hits per team is allowed.
d. A team rotates when it receives the service.
e. The ball is called dead when a foul occurs.

Fouls are:

1. A team allows the ball to hit the floor within its court.
2. A team propels the ball out of bounds and it hits the floor.
3. A player touches the net.
4. A player hits the ball before it crosses the net.
5. A player steps *across* the center line.
6. A player very obviously throws or lifts a ball.

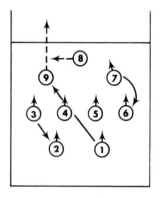

Figure 56

2. Modified Game

This particular game #2 emphasizes the fact that the last two hits per team should be the set passer and then the spiker. The "spiker" is the LF player and the "set passer" is the player immediately in front of her in court position. The last two hits must be #8 and then #9 (as in Figure 56). All other rules are the same as for "Modified Game" #1 above.

3. Modified Game

This particular game #3 emphasizes the fact that the last two hits per team should be the set passer and then the spiker, but the "spiker" is in a different position, RF, and the "set passer" is the player immediately behind her in court position. The last two hits must be #8 and then #7 (as in Figure 57). Other rules are the same as for "Modified Game" #1.

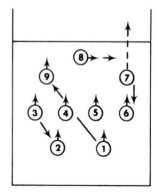

Figure 57

4. Modified Game

This game #4 reduces players to the regulation number of six. A point is scored each time:

a. The appropriate set passer (#3 in Figure 58) makes the *next to last* contact;

and

b. The appropriate spiker (#4 *or* #2 in Figure 58) makes the *last* hit.

All other rules are the same as for "Modified Game" #3. Each set passer should wear a colored penny so that team members can distinguish the set passers from the spikers.

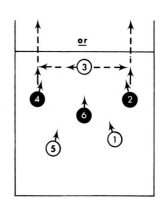

Figure 58

SUMMARY

1. Beginning and novice players can be discouraged by too stringent rules and regulations, whereas the skilled player is challenged by rigidly enforced regulations.
2. Players at all levels of skill should:
   a. Have fun in a game,
   b. Achieve some degree of success, and
   c. Be challenged to improve their skills without being threatened.
3. Modified games can be devised by the teacher to expedite the learning process.
4. Colored pennies can be used on the set passers to assist in building a concept of task assignment and assist players in instant location of spikers and set passers.

chapter 8

Teaching Progression

No two leaders will approach a group of volleyball players in the same manner. There is no one right way, with all others wrong. The criterion for judging method is success, and success is relative. Success means different things to different people. Each individual within the group, however, must receive satisfaction from her play experience.

AN APPROACH

A good progression takes into consideration principles underlying human behavior. The progression which follows is *an* approach to the learning process. The amount of time consumed by each of these steps will depend upon the group.

1. The players are given some idea of the game of volleyball—the objective is to get the ball into the opponents' court so that it will be difficult for its members to return the ball; a team scores a point or wins the service when the opposing team cannot return the ball.
2. The players are given instruction in a proper technique for sending the ball across the net—the overhand pass.
3. The players are drilled on this technique.
4. The players are briefed on the rules of "mass volleyball," and allowed to perform their newly-learned techniques in this game situation.
5. All players are given instruction in forward set passing. All players, even spikers, need to execute a set pass in a game situation. Beginner players may not know whether they want to train to become set passers or spikers.
6. Players are drilled briefly on forward set passing.
7. Players are briefed on the rules of Modified Game #1 and participate in it.
8. All players are given instruction in each of the various spiking progressions.

9. They are drilled on each progression.
10. Players are briefed on the rules of Modified Game #2 and participate in it.
11. All players are given instruction on all types of the service. Each individual's skill level will determine which type or types she can develop.
12. They are drilled on the service techniques.
13. Players are instructed in the use of underhand hitting.
14. Players drill on underhand hitting.
15. Players participate in Mass Volleyball. The teacher should emphasize good underhand techniques when that type of pass is necessary.
16. Players are instructed in proper footwork for playing in general situations. Figure 52 offers a simple drill for this practice.
17. The players are instructed in defensive formations or court positions for receiving the service and for covering vital areas on the service.
18. Players participate in Mass Volleyball and Modified Game #2, with particular emphasis on moving into position for overhand passing and using underhand hitting when absolutely necessary.
19. All players are given instruction in the other auxiliary skills of the one-hand overhead hit for distance, the one-fist overhead hit as a "save," the use of kneepads, recovering the ball from the net, and the use of verbal signals.
20. Players are drilled on these techniques.
21. Players participate in Mass Volleyball and Modified Game #2, with particular emphasis on the auxiliary skills in #19 above.
22. All players are instructed on coverage of vital areas when teammates are fielding a service, spiking, or passing.
23. Players are drilled on these formations. A drill follows each situation as it is presented.
24. Players are instructed in techniques for fielding spikes.
25. Players are drilled on techniques for fielding spikes.
26. All players are given instruction in the backward set pass.
27. Players are drilled in the backward set pass.
28. Players participate in Modified Game #3 and Modified Game #4.
29. All players are given instruction in the offensive pass and the dink.
30. Players are drilled in the execution of the offensive pass and the dink.
31. Players participate in a regulation game.
32. All players are given instruction in offensive formations utilizing four spikers and two set passers and coverage of vital areas.
33. Players are drilled on these formations.
34. Players participate in a regulation game, with particular emphasis on offensive formations.

35. All players are instructed in blocking and formations used for covering for blocking teammates.
36. Players are drilled in blocking and in formations used in covering for blocking teammates.

It is reiterated that the progression presented above is *an* approach. It is important that:

1. One remember that some skills are more difficult than others and take more time for development.
2. The skill and temperament of the group will dictate the amount of reinforcement and repetition necessary.
3. The teacher or coach will use her discretion regarding the proper time for introducing new techniques and the need for additional drilling on techniques already presented.
4. The skill level and interest of the particular group will determine whether or not all techniques included in this progression will be introduced.

WORKING WITH NOVICE AND MORE ADVANCED PLAYERS

If the members of the particular group being taught have already been introduced to the techniques of volleyball, are in various stages of individual skill development in the various techniques, and wish to move into "power volleyball," the leader must use methods to move the group and its individual members toward *advancement from their present status*. They must feel that they are learning new techniques or constructively improving their game before they will work conscientiously on drills. Treating them as rank beginners will detract from their enthusiasm.

An ideal teaching situation will involve two courts and four teams. At the beginning of the teaching unit the teacher can quickly determine the *general* skill status of the members of the group by arbitrarily putting them into four teams. This arbitrary placement can be accomplished by (1) asking players to place themselves in four groups of equal numbers (their choice of teammates), (2) having players in a circle and number off by fours with all the ones together, all twos together, etc., or (3) some other arbitrary method preferred by the leader. After the teams are thus established, the teams begin to play on the two courts and are instructed to play their very best game. This accomplishes two major objectives. (1) The players have an opportunity to *play* in a game situation which is their major objective. (2) The teacher can observe their individual and collective technique development.

The teams can be instructed that at the end of a specified time limit (ten minutes for example), the game will be completed and the team with more points wins the game. The teams can then be rotated on the courts so that each team has an opportunity to play each other team. The teacher thus has an opportunity to evaluate the present status of the group and can give the players her evaluation and the implications for a starting point for further instruction and specific technique drills. She can also involve the players in this evaluation of their performance.

The second session can be devoted to instruction in the technique(s) considered most appropriate for the group and skill drills involving this technique. The group can then be divided into four *different* arbitrary groups to repeat the round robin type of play, followed by evaluation and prescription of further activities to remove player weaknesses and promote advancement of skill.

This four team situation also gives the teacher an opportunity to group the players rather homogeneously by skill. The more skilled half of the players can be placed in two teams to play each other and the less skilled half of the group can be placed in two teams to play each other. In this manner the teacher can work on one court with the particular needs of that group while the other two teams play. Or she can work alternately with both groups, perhaps on different techniques. This is desirable from the point of view that *the teacher is responsible for providing a learning situation* in which *each person* can advance in knowledge and skill *if she desires to.* She is responsible to those who have devoted the time and energy to developing a high degree of skill as to those who have not had an opportunity to do so or have not assumed personal responsibility in learning situations as they were encountered. Pacing the learning situation to mediocrity is an abrogation of her responsibility to the more skilled. It is understandable of course that some or perhaps most of those in the less skilled half of the group may resent their "segregation." But it must be remembered also that two very unskilled players on a team with four relatively skilled players will definitely detract from the fun for the more skilled and also retard their progress in developing power volleyball skills. The teacher must bear in mind her responsibility to devote her professional attention to each group so that no player feels that she is being ignored or ostracized. It is difficult to achieve this objective. It is therefore desirable to alternate the homogeneous and heterogeneous groupings to help minimize the negative attitudes. One possibility is to use varied methods of arranging teams which is the framework within which players compete and also practice the various techniques and strategies comprising power volleyball. Examples of such team arrangement possibilities include:

1. The more skilled half of the group in two teams with the less skilled half in two teams as already described
2. The most skilled fourth of the group on one team, the next most skilled fourth on another team, and so on for each fourth
3. A heterogenous grouping of the various levels of skill on each team

This utilization of various groupings can serve to meet the varied objectives of:

1. Fun for the player in a competitive situation
2. Opportunities to work with teammates of similar skill level
3. Opportunities for the more skilled player to improve her skills by having assistance and psychological support of other skilled players
4. Opportunities for the less skilled player to work on her own level without impeding the progress of more advanced teammates, or, in some cases, without the interference of more skilled players who monopolize the activity
5. Opportunities for the more advanced players to assist the less skilled in ball handling and team strategy
6. Opportunities for the less skilled to enjoy the team play and excitement of playing with the more highly skilled and generally more enthusiastic players.

This alternation of groupings can be utilized (1) in skill drills on specific techniques or formations, (2) in daily scrimmages, (3) in class tournaments, etc. It is more desirable to have several tournaments within a power volleyball unit or course than to have only one tournament as a culmination. Various tournaments could be designed to incorporate the different groupings.

The rationale for the ideas presented above is basically that the teacher is professionally responsible to *each* person. It is her professional obligation to structure a learning situation which *can be* utilized productively and constructively by each person who *desires* to take advantage of it. This presupposes that the teacher is knowledgeable relative to techniques and strategies of power volleyball, that she can analyze individual and team performances, and that she can prescribe appropriate drills and other activities to keep the class moving always toward challenging and growth-promoting participation.

WORKING WITH LARGE NUMBERS IN A SMALL SPACE

Many teachers face a formidable problem by having too many students to allow each group a suitable space to engage in power volleyball on a regulation size court. Often this becomes a rationalization for having a volleyball type "free play" period with no meaningful instruction and no power volleyball techniques practiced. A conscientious teacher who is knowledgeable in the game of power volleyball can use her powers of improvisation to structure an environment conducive to learning even though the space is limited. The ideas which follow are only one approach. Each creative teacher can modify such ideas or follow her own.

To begin with, in developing techniques and strategies of power volleyball it is more important that there be six players on a team than that there be a regulation size court. With this concept in mind, a gymnasium structured to contain two regulation width courts could be set up with three nets, reducing the width of each; a gymnasium structured to contain one regulation court with excess space behind each end line could be set up so that three nets extend length wise down the room, reducing the width of each court slightly and reducing their length. The illustrations which follow diagram activities in a space in which three nets *could be* set up with reduced width and even possibly reduced length of each court.

Figure 59 diagrams ten activity stations for sixty students. Each of these drills are explained in detail in earlier chapters. Descriptions of the stations follow.

1. One hand overhead hit for distance: #6 tosses the ball about arm's length above the head of #1 who is standing about mid court; #1 executes a one hand overhead hit to the opposite backcourt
2. Dig over the net: #2 tosses a low ball to #1 who executes a backward dig to the opposite back court
3. Game situation
4. Spiking and set passing: #1 tosses the ball up and executes an overhand pass to #4; #4 executes a set pass; #1 approaches and spikes
5. One fist overhead as a save (a "punch"): #2 tosses a high ball which will not quite clear the net; #1 executes a one fist overhead hit
6. Wall spiking
7. Game situation
8. Spiking and set passing
9. Bump to a teammate: #4, #5, and #6 toss low balls to #1, #2, and #3 who bump the balls back to the passers in such a manner that the tosser has no difficulty in executing an overhand pass
10. Dig to a teammate: #6 tosses a low ball to #1; #1 executes a dig to #6; this dig should allow #6 to handle the ball with no difficulty; #6 sends the ball over the net into the backcourt with a backward pass. (In a game situation #6 could set pass to a spiker)

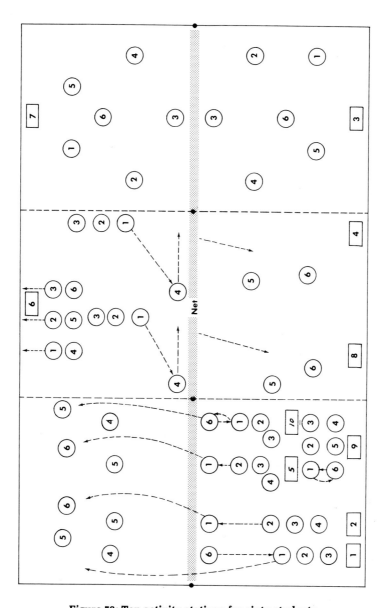

Figure 59: Ten activity stations for sixty students

Station numbers (in squares above) and description:

1. One hand overhead hit for distance   2. Dig over the net   3. Game situation
4. Spiking and set passing   5. One fist overhead as a save (a "punch")
6. Wall spiking   7. Game situation   8. Spiking and set passing
9. Bump to a teammate   10. Dig to a teammate

A team starting out at station one would successively engage in:

One hand overhead for distance
Dig over the net
A game
Spiking and set passing
One fist overhead as a save (a "punch")
Wall spiking
A game
Spiking and set passing
Bump to a teammate
Dig to a teammate

Each team not beginning at the number one station moves numerically to the next station. For example, if a team begins at station number 9, they move then to number 10, to number one, to number two, etc.

Figure 60 diagrams ten activity stations for sixty students.

1. Bump to a teammate: #3 and #6 toss a low ball to #1 and #4 who bump the ball back to the tosser so that she would have no difficulty in executing an overhand pass
2. Game situation
3. Serve against the wall: #1, #2, and #3 serve against the wall. A line on the wall at net height would give a visual indication of success
4. Game situation
5. Set pass into the basketball net: #3 and #6 toss the ball up and execute an overhand pass to #1 and #4 who execute a forward set pass, attempting to arc the ball so that it drops through the basketball net without touching the rim or the backboard
6. Dig to a teammate: #3 and #6 toss a low ball to #2 and #4 who execute a dig to the tosser, attempting to make it possible for the tosser to execute an overhand pass with little or no difficulty
7. Game situation
8. One hand overhead hit for distance: #3 and #6 toss a ball about arm's length above the heads of #1 and #4 who execute a one hand overhead hit against the wall high enough that it would clear the net and go into the opposing backcourt
9. Game situation
10. Wall spiking: #1, #2, and #3 hit the ball so that it contacts the floor, then the wall, and rebounds back to the spiker

A team starting at station number one would successively engage in:

Bump to a teammate
A game

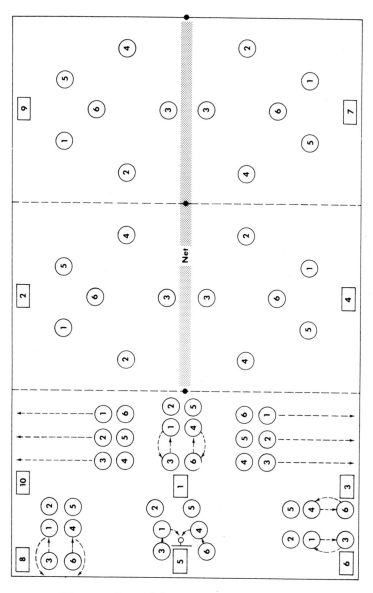

Figure 60: Ten activity stations for sixty students

Station numbers (in squares above) and description:

1. Bump to a teammate   2. Game situation   3. Serve against the wall
4. Game situation   5. Set pass into the basketball net   6. Dig to a teammate
7. Game situation   8. One hand overhead hit for distance   9. Game situation
10. Wall spiking

Serve against the wall
A game
Set pass
Dig to a teammate
A game
One hand overhead for distance
A game
Wall spiking

The station arrangement necessitates the teacher's giving adequate instruction in each drill and the appropriate execution of the technique involved prior to the implementation of the system to enable all players to work rather independently on each station assignment while she is then enabled to move about the room giving individualized attention. A responsible and capable team captain can be invaluable. A large diagram with station numbers and assignments accessible to the team captain and all players with a clear delineation of their starting position is necessary or much time can be wasted in getting organized at the time of each indicated change.

If students are careless or do not assume responsibilities adequately, there can be a safety hazard created by so many volleyballs in action. There are, however, enough players unoccupied at any given time in the technique drills that they can prevent most stray balls if they want to and are alert. More opportunities for actually hitting the ball enhance the possibilities for skill improvement. Standing around watching other people hit the ball most of the time is not as beneficial as actually hitting the ball the major portion of the activity session. And the financial cost of enough volleyballs is incidental in comparison with the wasted time and energy when students do not have equipment to work with.

chapter 9

A Typical Coaching Session

The selection of the content of any coaching session is determined by many factors such as the age and skill level of the players, the length of time they have played as a unit, how long they have been under the supervision of the particular coach, the length of the volleyball season, the past competition record, and the impending competition schedule.

The coaching session described in this chapter is designed for a team of relatively highly skilled players (older high school or college), in mid-season, with a nucleus of players who have played together several years with the same coach. They are familiar with the "system" of play advocated by the coach.

COACHING SESSION

The session consumes one and a half hours and includes the following activities:

1. Warm-up (approximately 7-10 minutes)
   a. Three slow laps around the gymnasium
   b. Partner passing
   c. Circle passing
   d. Shuttle passing
2. Skill drills
   a. Use of kneepads (Chapter 4)
   b. Underhand hitting (Figures 46, 47, 48, 49)
   c. Offensive pass (Figure 22)
   d. One-fist overhead hit as a "save" (Figure 51)
   e. One-hand overhead hit for distance (Figure 50) (a-e approximately 12-15 minutes)
   f. Spiking and set passing (Figure 10 and Figure 18, with spikers hitting from both LF and RF positions) (approximately 10 minutes)
   g. Blocking added to spiking and set passing (Figure 34) (approximately 10 minutes)
   h. Serving (approximately 5 minutes)

3. Discussion of team and individual weaknesses revealed in last competition. Discussion of individual and team strengths and weaknesses of team to be met at end of the week. (approximately 5 minutes)
4. Game participation with members of "A" and "B" teams intermixed though each spiker is teamed with her "regular" set passer.
   a. Strict officiating by a player who is not participating.
   b. Coach has a whistle which she uses to aid the student official in stringently enforcing rules and to stop play for "coaching opportunities." (approximately 15 minutes)
5. Game participation with "A" team competing against "B" team. (approximately 17-20 minutes)
6. Group conference
   a. Ask players to volunteer comments relative to evaluation of the session.
   b. Coach points out major strengths observed;
   c. Coach points out major weaknesses observed;
   d. Coach congratulates any outstanding individual or group progress observed during the session. (approximately 3-5 minutes)
7. Showers

COACHING SUGGESTIONS

1. The skill of a team as a unit is dependent upon each individual's development of skill in the fundamental techniques; each coaching session should emphasize some of these techniques. Players can move quickly from one drill to another on the coach's signal once they are familiar with the drills.
2. Individual player, team, and coach diagnosis and evaluation should be continuous.
3. Intermixing "A" and "B" teams helps in developing squad depth and unity, gives opportunity for success in a game situation for less skilled players, and offers a more competitive situation.
4. Competition of "A" against "B" teams gives the necessary practice in team unity and understanding of each player's relationship to her teammates.
5. Use every means and opportunity to develop and maintain a high level *espirit de corps.*
6. Supervision and coaching from the side line by the teacher should be constant, supportive, and analytical.
   a. Assist the student official with stringent enforcement of rules. It is better to enter competition accustomed to such officiating; it is

easier for a team to adjust to less stringent officiating should they encounter it.

    b. Pitch the voice low and talk as the students participate in all aspects of the activity session; acknowledge good plays and call instructions when needed. Stop play; point out weaknesses in formation (exposure of vital areas), their cause, and the possible consequences. Move onto the court and place players into position if necessary.

    c. Take advantage of all "coaching moments" to help students gain insight into their functioning or lack of it.

7. The content of a coaching session depends upon many factors.

    a. The coach should strive to engage in a constant process of increasing:

        1. Her knowledge of the game,

        2. Her knowledge and implementation of the theories of learning,

        3. Her understanding of the personality and motivations of each individual team member,

        4. Her understanding of the dynamics of the particular group,

        5. Her ability to diagnose individual and team strengths and weaknesses relative to volleyball techniques,

        6. Her ability to transpose her observations into activities that are meaningful in developing additional individual and team competencies and increased student awareness and insight.

    b. The coach must develop a clear concept of the "system" of play she advocates, and use systematic progressions to achieve this end; she may adjust it for any of a variety of reasons, but the students should always have a clear idea of what is expected of them.

    c. Some suggestions for alteration in the general procedure described in the coaching session presented in this chapter include:

        1. Younger players might spend less time in a session; they might have one skill technique introduced, spend more time with it, and spend the major portion of the session participating in one or more of the modified games.

        2. A relatively skilled group with a "new" coach might spend the majority of a session on drills designed to develop offensive and defensive formations necessitated by the coach's "system."

SUMMARY

1. The selection of the content of any coaching session is determined by many factors.

2. The activities selected should have meaning and significance for the players at that particular time.
3. The session outlined in this chapter is appropriate for a group of relatively highly skilled players and a nucleus of girls who have progressed with the same coach for several years.
4. The session includes warm-up activities, drills on several fundamental skills, group discussion consisting of diagnosis and evaluation, game participation, and showering.
5. Coaching suggestions emphasize:
    a. Careful selection of the contents of the session;
    b. Continuous individual, team, and coach diagnosis and evaluation;
    c. Development of *espirit de corps;*
    d. Constant analytical and supportive supervision and teaching;
    e. Continuous growth and development of the coach's own competency to analyze pertinent factors, transpose her knowledge into significant and meaningful activity, and evaluate outcomes; and
    f. Structure of the coaching session content for *individuals* and a *specific group.*

chapter 10

The Psychology of Coaching

The successful coach may not be at home in a psychological laboratory but she has acquainted herself with important facts about human behavior; her success is due in no small measure to this knowledge. She is in every sense of the word a teacher. As a teacher she is aware of some of the general principles concerning human behavior.

First, she recognizes that individual differences exist among girls and women with whom she will work. Successful coaching and teaching involve helping every girl realize her full capacities, giving every girl tasks commensurate with her talents, and helping each one to be successful in contributing to the team. Second, she knows that the spirit of play appears to be an unlearned disposition. Third, because of the natural playfulness of youth the coach recognizes that she will be successful in proportion to her own youthful spirit and perception of the longings and desires of the young she teaches. Adults tend to harden, to lose perspective of their younger days, to crystallize, to become unsympathetic, to forget the vagaries and wistfulness of their own adolescence; they tend to move completely out of the days of youth into the harder, more critical, more unemotional days of maturity. As a result they become less effective in guiding young people. Youngsters and adolescents are plastic, soft, emotional, jealous, eager, enthusiastic, prejudiced, full of abandonment, tirelessness, and resilience. Fourth, she understands that as we grow we acquire habits and we learn under the direction of parents, peers, neighbors, and teachers—habits of feeling, modes of thinking, and types of personal and social action.

The coach is a teacher and she must share all she knows of plays, formations, signal systems, types of skill, strategy, and rules of the game. She has great power to influence the character formation of those she teaches. Perhaps the greatest objective in coaching is to contribute to the attainment of a fighting mind and a skillful and efficient body, first in games but finally in the game of life. The coach must have confidence in the dignity of her profession, must know the sport she teaches, must understand human physiology and psychology, and must know something about the functioning of the intellect.

SOME PSYCHOLOGICAL PRINCIPLES

Instruction and practice sessions must be carefully planned if the time spent is to be profitable. This means that the principles of learning should be utilized. This requires that:

1. There is a proper and favorable length for a practice period. Continued practice of any one skill without adequate rest leads to ineffective repetitions.
2. Practice on a new skill twice in one day may be advantageous when the skill is first introduced; after the first few practice periods once a day is sufficient; in the later stages of learning, practice of a skill once every two or three days is just as effective if not more effective than daily practice.
3. The learning of *complicated* skills is more rapid if skills are broken down into meaningful fundamentals. Practice is most effective when the fundamentals are real and not artificial segments of the game. Practice on fundamentals must be supplemented by frequent practice periods devoted to actual playing of the game.
4. The emotional state of the learner affects her practice in a profound way. A state of annoyance, displeasure, discomfort, distaste, sullenness, anger, fear, and the like may retard learning.
5. The rate of learning depends in part on the way in which material is presented.
6. Learning is a process that takes time. Endless repetition on one or two days is futile. "Cramming" is a wasteful method of attempting to become skillful. Practice should be distributed over a period of time.
7. Rate of learning is influenced by *intent to learn*. The individual must resolve to make progress in acquiring skill; she must concentrate to keep herself at a high level of earnestness. Practice for limited periods of time with this frame of mind contributes to maximum progress in skill acquisition. Players often reach a practical degree of skill and call it their best. Renewed intent to acquire additional skill may sometimes be gained by seeing a real artist at work.
8. Rate of learning is influenced by one's incentives to practice. Incentives to practice may come from an approaching competitive game or the hope of winning a championship; the coach must use great discretion in imposing these particular incentives. Players derive motives also from rivalry with a teammate or from friendships, home life, and school life. This incentive may come from a knowledge of the end

sought; that is, when an individual knows the degree of skill required to "make the team," she may be motivated to acquire that skill. Knowledge of the relationship of a skill or a strategy to the game as a whole rather than ignorance of its relationship contributes incentive to practice a segment. Knowledge of one's scores or progress and errors during the process of learning results in perseverance.

9. Rest and relaxation affect the rate of learning. We rest when we sleep, when we are awake but completely relaxed, and when we turn from one task to another.

The conduct of practice periods has significance in terms of outcomes. Learners should be supported by good equipment and good management. Congenial girls should be grouped together. Each practice period should be distinctive. The coach must use ingenuity in inventing new things to do, new ways of doing old things, new stories to tell, and new and effective ways of maintaining interest.

The successful coach must present material effectively. Knowledge possessed by the coach who was a great athlete is inconsequential if she cannot present her facts to others effectively. Some factors relative to effective presentation of material include:

1. Most persons are visually-minded but athletes learn to make extensive use of muscular or kinesthetic perceptions. All diagrams and illustrations should be supplemented by actual working through the play and the formations or the movements that are diagrammed.
2. Learning is helped a great deal by the actual performance of a new skill and by adapting that skill to the natural traits of the learner.
3. Every new task must appear to be a genuine part of the total game.
4. The fundamentals which are *learned* are supported by exceptions and incidentals which are to be *remembered*. These exceptions are memorized and not automatized.
5. All tasks must be adapted to the mental level of the players concerned.
6. "Cramming" as a method of learning is at its best when the cramming period is a review or a period of relearning.

The season must be carefully planned. A schedule should be made with care. The judgment of the coach should be influenced by broad principles of strategy and by an understanding of the capacities of the players rather than by a desire to impress the world with her skill as a coach or by the venom of an ancient rivalry. Some of the considerations in planning the season include:

1. Keep a free and easy spirit of play within the group from the beginning to the end of the season.

2. A good way to keep skill at a high level is to grant many rest days, particularly in the latter part of the season.
3. A winning streak is due in part to chance. It may be broken by over-confidence, too much hard work, losing a natural leader on the team, or breaking training.
4. A "green" team cannot play the same schedule as a team of "veterans."
5. Teams are overcoached when the coach tries to force her style of play upon others, when players are talked to too much, and when they are pushed too frequently to an emotional extreme.
6. Staleness can be avoided by rest.
7. When players are alert, eager, delicately coordinated, steady, and enthusiastic they are at the height of their training. The coach must learn to "feel" such a state of readiness by paying attention to little details in the reactions of players.
8. Overconfidence is characterized by a dislike for details, unwilling-ness to exert oneself, and by inability to keep events in proper perspective.
9. The coach can avoid overconfidence by magnifying the play spirit, by refusing to make too much of star players, and by controlling publicity.
10. Anxiety and foreboding usually are products of ignorance and are avoided by keeping players busy and attending to familiar tasks.
11. Bodily expressions of anger and fear are signs of profound internal changes which can make an athlete more capable of prolonged and intense work, and can be dissipated thereby.
12. Fear can be controlled by getting into action as soon as possible, by turning one's attention to the desires or problems of others, and by going through some well-habituated performance. The coach and the captain are responsible for controlling fear in the group.

The really significant aspects of the game take place in the minds of the players, the captain, and the coach. The coach on the sideline looks through the disorder—even the skill—to the spirits of the players. What is the spiker or set passer planning now? Have the players seen strategic moments in the game? Have they judged the temper of the opponents correctly? Have they found the fatigued body or wandering mind on the opposing team? Is that spiker playing her role well enough to deceive the opponents in her intentions? Is our morale still greater than theirs? What influence did the last poor play have upon the spirit of the team? Will the team relax because it is ahead?

Morale or spirit is an intangible mental attitude. High morale affects the individual mentally and physically so that she is capable of any task. It is a mental condition characterized by the ability to "come back"; it is mental and physical integrity and can be contrasted to the lethargic and melancholy mind. It is not a free and uncontrolled optimism—a cheerful kind of idiocy. It is not mere crowd emotionalism although coaches frequently make the error of supposing that it is. Morale is more important than any other single factor in a competitive game. A team can defeat itself much more quickly than can its opponents. We are all familiar with the highly skilled team defeated by a team far less skilled.

In the joy of a victory in the second game that comes after a lost first game in the match, a spectator will probably forget what took place in the three minutes between the first and second games. Three minutes do not allow enough time to build new strength or new game skills; it is long enough, however, to get a *new outlook*. More than one team beaten unmercifully in the first game has returned reborn in its mind.

SUGGESTIONS FOR BUILDING MORALE

Suggestions for developing specific skills and strategies have been given throughout this book. Many are pertinent in building morale. Other suggestions include:

1. Relieve tension by taking time out for group conference, running a lap between games, circle passing between games, etc.
2. Talking and clapping the hands during play is beneficial. Players should encourage dispirited teammates and congratulate good plays. Call plays occasionally and aid teammates by calling "out!"
3. The pregame warm-up session can do much to give a team a psychological advantage if its members perform well and the opponents are impressed with their abilities.
4. An all-out effort which results in the winning of the first game of the match can give a psychological advantage.
5. Do not relax or reduce the level of efficiency if the opponents have fewer points at any given time. Press any advantage.
6. The coach must express confidence in the team and lend her decisive support from the side line.
7. The team must have some kind of "system" for determining when the captain will call a time out when a demoralizing situation occurs, for example, when three points are lost in quick succession.
8. Pre-tournament matches should be arranged for the team. At the college level in particular, teams too often participate in tournaments without prior competitive experience.

SUMMARY

1. Successful coaching necessitates consideration of individual differences, taking advantage of the natural play spirit, maintenance of a youthful spirit in the personality of the coach, and guiding the student's formation of habits.
2. Practice improves skills only when there is:
   a. Wise use in repetition of the same drill;
   b. Proper length of practice sessions;
   c. Complicated skills are divided into segments;
   d. Time devoted to actual playing of the game;
   e. Recognition of the effect of an individual's emotions upon her performance;
   f. Practice over a period of time rather than "cramming";
   g. Intent to learn;
   h. Incentives to practice;
   i. Sufficient rest and relaxation.
3. Each practice period should be distinctive.
4. The coach should give attention to details in planning a practice session.
5. Material to be learned must be presented effectively:
   a. The coach should reenforce visual presentations with actual movement through formations;
   b. The form of a technique should be adapted to the individual's natural traits;
   c. Segments which are practiced must be authentic parts of the game;
   d. Fundamental techniques should be automatized and exceptions remembered;
   e. Tasks must be adapted to the mental level of the individual; and
   f. Cramming is most effective as review and for relearning purposes.
6. The planning of a volleyball season should be based on the capacities of the players and a broad strategy:
   a. It should be fun;
   b. Rest days should be allowed, for they help in maintaining a high efficiency level;
   c. A winning streak can be broken by the coach's poor planning or players' carelessness;
   d. Inexperienced players must be nurtured;
   e. The team should not be overcoached;
   f. Overconfidence can be recognized by certain characteristics and can be controlled by the coach;
   g. Anxiety can be relieved;

    h. The player's anger can be used to her advantage; and

    i. Fear is natural but the coach should plan activities to combat it.

7. The real significance of the sport of volleyball is the effect it has upon the participants; the outcome is measured in terms of its contribution to individual personality.

8. An intangible mental attitude called morale or spirit is more important than any other single factor (even skill) in a team's performance.

9. The coach must make a concerted effort to develop and maintain a high degree of morale throughout the season of practice and in all competitive situations. Some suggestions include:

    a. Relieve tension and fear with constructive activity;

    b. Players can aid each other in achieving and maintaining a high level of morale;

    c. Gain a psychological advantage by a good pregame performance;

    d. Make an all-out effort to win the first game of a match;

    e. Press any advantage over an opponent;

    f. Active and decisive support of the coach on the side line is important;

    g. A "system" should be determined to arrest a temporary demoralizing climate in a game; and

    h. Participation in competition prior to a tournament.

chapter 11

The Future of Power Volleyball

It was pointed out in Chapter 1 that the game of volleyball is an infant of seventy years in comparison with many universal games two thousand or more years old. Nevertheless, it enjoys great popularity among the peoples of the world and is one of the most rapidly growing team games. Its international popularity is evidenced by its inclusion in the Olympic Games and the Pan American Games. Its popularity in the United States is indicated by the growing number of college varsity teams, increasing extramural competition at the college level, growing numbers of competitive teams of high school boys and girls, and the significant increase in numbers and competencies of men and women competing in the USVBA National Championships.

This growth has been the result of the dedicated and tireless efforts of enthusiasts of the game. Clinics organized and presented by individuals affiliated with DGWS and USVBA have contributed immeasurably to increased knowledge and skill. More extramural competition among college women has exposed teachers, coaches, and players to advanced skills and techniques and has fostered interest among highly-skilled individuals who were previously interested only in basketball. This interest is progressive in effect. Many of the women competing in extramural competition are physical education majors and eventually will go into public schools and colleges better equipped to teach and coach power volleyball and to further their own knowledge through reading, attending clinics, interviewing, and experimenting with their students.

The increased popularity of volleyball has come about in part, if not primarily, because of the influence power volleyball has had on individuals who have participated in it as players, teachers, recreation leaders, spectators, etc., and as a result of the promotion of the sport by the DGWS and the USVBA. This interest will in all probability grow and perhaps even mushroom.

The skills in power volleyball are going through an evolutionary process just as basketball skills did and still are, but to a lesser degree. As the popularity of basketball increased, players and coaches refined techniques and methods of teaching the skills and they learned by emulation and experimentation. Changes in basketball skills today are not as rapid or revolutionary as they once were. Skillful Americans participating in national and international power volleyball competitions also learn by emulation and return to their communities to teach the new techniques. Players and coaches participating in international competition learn from their competitors and then disseminate their knowledge; they experiment to develop improved playing techniques and methods of teaching and to develop more functional rules.

The past history and present rapid growth of power volleyball point toward a future in which it will have increased popularity and more highly skilled participants. Suggestions to speed this process include:

1. Clinics for players, teachers, coaches, recreation leaders, prospective teachers and coaches, and other interested persons should be conducted by qualified persons. Through clinics additional potential enthusiasts can be reached.
2. Publicity at the local and national level can educate the public about power volleyball. National television coverage of expert play can widen the horizon of many players and their coaches.
3. Films and filmstrips developed by competent persons can aid in disseminating knowledge concerning power volleyball.
4. The inclusion of volleyball in a state's interscholastic league structure at the state tournament level can equate its stature with that of basketball, football, softball, tennis, and other sports.
5. Intercollegiate competition for men and women can give volleyball players incentive for further development.
6. One set of rules for all players could be of great value.

glossary

AAHPER—American Association for Health, Physical Education, and Recreation

Attack—team offense; the ball moves from the original receiver, to the set passer, to the spiker

Backs—players in back court positions; left, center, and right backs

Backward set pass—the set passer passes the ball behind her to the spiker who should be there

Blocking—a technique employed by one or more players to impede the progress of a spiked ball

Bump—also called the forearm pass; an underhand hit, usually to a teammate, in which the ball is contacted with both extended forearms while the hands are clasped together

Change of pace—changing the tempo of a player's movements; changing the tempo of the game by using a variety of techniques (using an offensive pass rather than a set pass to the spiker)

Cover—to protect an area of the court

DGWS—Division for Girls and Women's Sports (division of AAHPER)

Dead ball—a ball no longer in play because it has been played illegally; point, side out, or a replay occurs when the ball is dead

Defense—the attempt to gain control of the ball in order to become the offensive team; fielding a spiked or well-placed ball

Dig pass—an underhand technique used to field low balls with one hand

Dink—a technique used to direct the ball over the hands or to the side of the blockers

Double foul—players on opposing teams commit fouls simultaneously

Fielding—recovering a ball spiked or passed from the opposing team

Floater service—a variation of the overhead service which has no spin and weaves in its flight

Forearm pass—see "bump"

Formation—a defensive or offensive arrangement of players into a functional pattern

Forward set pass—the set passer passes the ball in the direction she is facing; the spiker is in front of her

Foul—the violation of a rule; in USVBA rules there are fouls and errors, and a foul takes precedence over an error

Give with the ball—relax the extended hands to allow them to move backward on contact with the ball; allows for absorption of some of the speed and shock of impact

Holding—a delayed action in handling the ball; the ball must be batted; it must leave the hands immediately after contact

Kill—a hard-driven spike which is difficult or impossible for the opponents to return

Match—two out of three games

Modified game—a game played under rules other than the official DGWS or USVBA rules; the rules are adapted to serve a specific purpose; modification offers a framework for play involving skill progressions

Offense—possession of the ball; advancing the ball for set passing and spiking

Offensive pass—a technique used by an offensive player to send the ball to the opponents' court when she sees an opportunity to catch them out of position

"Off side" of the spiker—ideally, a set pass for a right handed spiker should come from her right side and from the left side of a left handed spiker. "Off side" means the opposite; that is, a right handed spiker receives a set pass from her left side. This is more difficult for the spiker

One-fist overhead as a "save"—a technique used by a forward when the teammate's pass cannot be advantageously handled otherwise

One-foot takeoff—a spiker approaches the net and springs upward from one foot

One-hand overhead for distance—a pass used by a player when the ball is too high overhead for the overhand pass

Overhand pass—the technique used most frequently to move the ball to a teammate; two hands moving forward and upward contact the ball; the backs of the hands are toward the face

Pass—to move the ball from one player to another or toward the opponents' court

Point—a score given to the serving team when the receiving team plays illegally

Position—the space occupied by a player; some are specifically designated by lines or imaginary lines on the floor; others are designated by strategy

Power volleyball—a game involving twelve individually skilled players with specific responsibilities maneuvering in definite, planned, and strategic offensive and defensive patterns; it is volleyball played with more precision, more strategy, more advanced techniques, more color and skill—more "power"—than is observed in most volleyball games

Progression—a succession of movements or segments of a technique beginning with less difficult skills and building up to more difficult patterns

"Punch"—See one-fist overhead as a "save"

Rally—the play starting with the service and ending with the point, side out, or dead ball

Receiver—a player who is to handle a ball

Rotation—the movement of a team in its serving order; players move one position clockwise when side out is called and their team begins to serve

Service—the act of putting the ball into play after point, side out, or a dead ball

Serving area—the space behind the end line extending from the court's right side line ten feet toward the center of the court

Service placement—serving the ball in such a manner that it moves to a predetermined position on the opponents' court

Set pass—a pass positioned so that it can be spiked; usually the second pass in the series by the offensive team

Set passer—the player who passes the ball to the spiker in such a manner that it can be spiked

Side out—loss of the service by a team

Spike—occurs when the ball is hit downward with force into the opponents' court; it is the "kill" play of the game

Spiker—the player whose offensive duty is to spike the ball

Spiking line—a line on the court ten feet from and parallel to the center line

Strategy—a planned act or series of acts considered useful in defeating the opponent or using the individual players involved in the most advantageous manner

Switch—two or more players simultaneously change positions

Timing—the regulation of movement; an accelerating or slowing of the body or the ball to make the execution of a technique ideal

Take-off from two feet—a spiker approaches the net, jumps forward slightly, and springs upward from both feet simultaneously

Underhand hitting—this technique should not be used unless it is absolutely necessary; the back of the player's hand or hands is toward the floor

USVBA—United States Volleyball Association

Verbal signals—players inform officials and teammates of a situation
that exists at the moment; it is pertinent to the game; it has significance for the officials or the teammates

Vital area—a part of the court where the ball might possibly be handled
next; it is advantageous for the team to pattern its movements to protect this area; it varies with the offensive and defensive situation

Volley—see pass

Warm-up—movements or exercises designated to prepare the individual
physiologically and psychologically for play

Wall spiking—a drill for developing spiking arm movements; a player
tosses the ball, spikes it against the floor so that the ball bounces off
the floor, against the wall, and back toward the player

Results of National
and International Competition

Women's National Intercollegiate Volleyball Championships conducted by the Association for Intercollegiate Athletics for Women (AIAW) and the Division of Girls' and Women's Sports (of the AAHPER).

No. Year	Place	Winners
*1. 1970	California State College, Long Beach	1. Sul Ross State Univ. (Texas) 2. Univ. of Cal. at Los Angeles 3. San Diego State College 4. Cal. State College at Long Beach Consolation: Univ. of Southern Cal.
**2. 1971	University of Kansas, Lawrence	1. Sul Ross State Univ. 2. Cal. State College at Long Beach 3. Southwest Texas State Univ. 4. Univ. of Oregon 5. Miami-Dade Junior College 6. Southwest Missouri State
**3. 1972	Miami-Dade Junior College, Miami, Florida	1. Univ. of Cal. at Los Angeles 2. Cal. State College at Long Beach 3. San Fernando Valley State College 4. Univ. of Cal. at Santa Barbara 5. Sul Ross State Univ.
***3. 1973	Brigham Young Univ. Provo, Utah	1 Cal. State College at Long Beach 2. Brigham Young Univ. 3. Univ. of Cal. at Los Angeles 4. Southwest Texas State Univ. 5. Church College of Hawaii

* Information obtained from Dixie Grimmett, Women's Physical Education, California State College, Long Beach.
** Information obtained from DGWS office, Washington, D.C.
*** Information obtained from Elaine Michaelis, Meet Director, Brigham Young University.

The charts which follow appear through the permission of Dr. Harold T. Friermood who compiles the results of tournaments each year and publishes them in the *USVBA Official Guide*. The charts will give the reader an idea of the location of American volleyball "powers" and the relative position of the United States in international competition.

WINNER OF NATIONAL (USVBA) WOMEN'S VOLLEYBALL CHAMPIONSHIPS

No.	Year	Place	Winner	Runner-up
1.	1949	Los Angeles, Cal. Downtown YMCA & Naval Reserve Armory	Houston, Texas "Eagles"	Los Angeles, Cal., L. A. Training Academy
2.	1950	Knoxville, Tenn. Chilhowee Park YMCA	Santa Monica, Cal., "Voit No. 1"	Houston, Texas, "Red Shields"
3.	1951	Springfield College Springfield, Mass.	Houston, Texas "Eagles"	Houston, Texas, "Red Shields"
4.	1952	Columbus, Ohio Ohio State Univ.	Santa Monica, Cal. "Voit No. 1"	Santa Monica, Cal., "Wahines"
5.	1953	Omaha, Neb., YMCA & Boys Town	Los Angeles, Cal., "Voit No. 1"	Houston, Texas, "Red Shields"
6.	1954	Tucson, Ariz. YMCA and H.S.	Houston, Texas Houstonettes	Houston, Texas, "Red Shields"
7.	1955	Oklahoma City, Okla. YMCA	Santa Monica, Cal., Mariners	Houston, Texas, "Red Shields"
8.	1956	Seattle, Wash. YMCA	Santa Monica, Cal., Mariners	Houston, Texas, La Rose Houstonettes
9.	1957	Memphis, Tenn. YMCA at Millington Naval Air Station	Santa Monica, Cal., Mariners	Houston, Texas La Rose Houstonettes
10.	1958	Scranton, Pa. YMCA	Santa Monica, Cal., "Mariners"	Long Beach, Cal., "Challengers"
11.	1959	Des Moines, Iowa YMCA (No. Side H.S.)	Santa Monica, Cal., "Mariners"	Long Beach, Cal., "Challengers"
12.	1960	Dallas, Texas YMCA (at S. M. U.)	Santa Monica, Cal., "Mariners"	Los Angeles, Cal., "Genies"
13.	1961	Duluth, Minn. At U. M. D.	Long Beach, Cal., "Breakers"	Dallas, Texas, YMCA
14.	1962	Phila. Palestra	Long Beach Ahern's	Dallas YMCA
15.	1963	San Antonio, Texas	Long Beach Ahern's	Los Angeles Spartans
16.	1964	New York City Met. YMCA at Queens College	Los Angeles, Cal. Ahern Shamrocks	Los Angeles, Cal. Renegades
17.	1965	Omaha, Neb. Offutt Air Force Base	Los Angeles, Cal. Shamrocks	Los Angeles, Cal. South Bay Cities Triumph
18.	1966	Grand Rapids, Mich. YMCA at Calvin College	Los Angeles, Cal. Renegades	Long Beach, Cal. Ahern Shamrocks
19.	1967	Detroit, Mich. Met. YMCA at Wayne State Univ.	Long Beach, Cal. Shamrocks	Los Angeles, Cal. Renegade Green
20.	1968	Portland, Oregon YMCA at Portland State Col.	Long Beach, Cal. Shamrocks	Los Angeles, Cal. Renegade Blues

WINNERS OF NATIONAL YMCA VOLLEYBALL CHAMPIONSHIPS

No.	Year	Place	Winner	Runner-up
1.	1922	Brooklyn, N.Y. Central YMCA	Pittsburgh, Pa., Downtown YMCA	Germantown, Pa., YMCA
2.	1923	Chicago, Ill. Hyde Park YMCA	Pittsburgh, Pa., Downtown YMCA	Aurora, Ill., YMCA
3.	1924	Pittsburgh, Pa. Downtown YMCA	Pittsburgh, Pa., Downtown YMCA	Germantown, Pa., YMCA
4.	1925	Des Moines, Iowa YMCA	Pittsburgh, Pa., Downtown YMCA	Fort Wayne, Ind. YMCA
5.	1926	Philadelphia, Pa. Central YMCA	Pittsburgh, Pa., Downtown YMCA	Germantown, Pa., YMCA
6.	1927	Fort Wayne, Ind. YMCA	Chicago, Ill. Hyde Park YMCA	Pittsburgh, Pa., YMCA
7.	1928	Chattanooga, Tenn. YMCA	Germantown, Pa. YMCA	Chicago, Ill., Hyde Park YMCA
8.	1929	Chicago, Ill. Hyde Park YMCA	Chicago, Ill., Hyde Park YMCA	Chicago, Ill., Division St. YMCA
9.	1930	Columbus, Ohio Central YMCA	Chicago, Ill., Hyde Park YMCA	Denver, Colo., YMCA
10.	1931	Rochester, N.Y. Central YMCA	San Antonio, Texas, YMCA	Chicago, Ill. Division St. YMCA
11.	1932	Chicago, Ill. Hyde Park YMCA	San Antonio, Texas, YMCA	Chicago, Ill., Hyde Park YMCA
12.	1933	Chicago, Ill. Conducted by YMCA at Naval Reserve Armory	Houston, Texas, YMCA	Chicago, Ill., Hyde Park YMCA
13.	1934	Knoxville, Tenn. YMCA	Houston, Texas, YMCA	Chicago, Ill., Division St. YMCA
14.	1935	Binghamton, N.Y. YMCA	Houston, Texas, YMCA	Chicago, Ill., Division St. YMCA
15.	1936	Davenport, Iowa YMCA	Houston, Texas YMCA	Philadelphia, Pa., Central Br. YMCA
16.	1937	Louisville, Ky. YMCA	Chicago, Ill., Duncan YMCA	Philadelphia, Pa., North Br. YMCA
17.	1938	Detroit, Mich. Downtown YMCA	Houston, Texas, YMCA	Davenport, Iowa YMCA
18.	1939	San Francisco, Cal. Embarcadero YMCA	Houston, Texas, YMCA	Chicago, Ill., North Avenue YMCA
19.	1940	Philadelphia, Pa. Central YMCA and Penn. AC	Houston, Texas, YMCA	San Francisco, Cal., Embarcadero YMCA
20.	1941	Ann Arbor, Mich. YMCA at Univ. of Mich. Intramural Sports Bldg.	Chicago, Ill., North Ave., Larrabee YMCA	Houston, Texas, YMCA
21.	1946	Chicago, Ill. At Hyde Park YMCA and Univ. of Chicago	Pasadena, Cal., YMCA	Houston, Texas, YMCA
22.	1947	Houston, Tex. At YMCA and Coliseum	Chicago, Ill. , North Ave., Larrabee YMCA	Pasadena, Cal., YMCA

No.	Year	Place	Winner	Runner-up
23.	1948	South Bend, Ind. At YMCA and John Adams High School	Hollywood, Cal., YMCA	Los Angeles, Cal., Downtown YMCA
24.	1949	Los Angeles, Cal. By Downtown and Hollywood YMCA's at Naval Reserve Armory	Los Angeles, Cal., Downtown YMCA	Long Beach, Cal., YMCA
25.	1950	Knoxville, Tenn. YMCA, Chilhowee Park	Long Beach, Cal., YMCA	Hollywood, Cal., YMCA
26.	1951	Springfield, Mass. Springfield College	Hollywood, Cal., YMCA	Chicago, Ill., North Ave. YMCA
27.	1952	Columbus, Ohio Ohio State Univ.	Hollywood, Cal., YMCA	Stockton, Cal., YMCA
28.	1953	Omaha, Nebraska YMCA	Hollywood, Cal., YMCA	Long Beach, Cal., YMCA
29.	1954	Tucson, Ariz. YMCA and High School	Stockton, Cal., YMCA	Hollywood, Cal., YMCA Stars
30.	1955	Oklahoma City, Okla. YMCA	Stockton, Cal., YMCA	Hollywood, Cal., YMCA Stars
31.	1956	Seattle, Wash. YMCA	Hollwood, Cal., YMCA Stars	Stockton, Cal., YMCA
32.	1957	Memphis, Tenn. YMCA at Millington Naval Air Station	Hollywood, Cal., YMCA Stars	Stockton, Cal., YMCA
33.	1958	Scranton, Pa. YMCA	Hollywood, Cal., YMCA Stars	Chicago, Ill., Wilson Ave. Dept. YMCA
34.	1959	Des Moines, Iowa YMCA	Hollywood, Cal., YMCA Stars	Stockton, Cal., YMCA
35.	1960	Dallas, Texas YMCA at S. M. U.	Hollywood, Cal., YMCA Stars	Stockton, Cal., YMCA
36.	1961	Duluth, Minn. At U. M. D.	Hollywood YMCA	Stockton, Cal., YMCA
37.	1962	Phila. Palestra	Hollywood YMCA	Pasadena YMCA
38.	1963	San Antonio, Texas	Hollywood YMCA	Stockton YMCA
39.	1964	New York City Met. YMCA at Queens College	Hollywood, Cal., YMCA Stars	Hollywood, Cal. YMCA Comets
40.	1965	Omaha, Neb. Offutt Air Force Base	Los Angeles, Cal. Downtown YMCA	Chicago, Ill. Lawson YMCA
41.	1966	Grand Rapids, Mich. YMCA at Calvin College	Los Angeles, Cal. Downtown YMCA	Stockton, Cal. YMCA
42.	1967	Detroit, Mich. Met. YMCA at Wayne State Col.	Los Angeles, Cal. Downtown YMCA	Dallas, Texas Downtown YMCA
43.	1968	Portland, Oregon YMCA at Portland State College	Los Angeles, Cal. Downtown YMCA	Long Beach, Cal. YMCA

WINNERS OF NATIONAL (USVBA) ARMED FORCES
VOLLEYBALL CHAMPIONSHIPS

No.	Year	Place	Winner	Runner-up
1.	1952	Columbus, Ohio Ohio State Univ.	Los Alamitos Naval Air Station, Los Alamitos, Cal.	Pensacola, Fla., Whiting Field Naval Air Station
2.	1953	Omaha, Neb. YMCA and Boys Town	Los Alamitos Naval Air Station, Los Alamitos, Cal.	Hamilton, Cal., Air Force Base
3.	1954	Tucson, Ariz. YMCA and High School	Hamilton, Cal., Air Force Base	Los Alamitos, Cal., Los Alamitos Naval Air Station
4.	1955	Oklahoma City, Okla. YMCA	Los Alamitos Naval Air Station, Los Alamitos, Cal.	Hamilton, Cal., Air Force Base
5.	1956	Seattle, Wash. YMCA	Hamilton, Cal., Air Force Base	San Francisco, Cal., Presidio 6th Army Base
6.	1957	Memphis, Tenn. YMCA at Millington Naval Air Station	Houston, Texas, Ellington Air Force Base	Los Alamitos Naval Air Station, Los Alamitos, Cal.
7.	1958	Scranton, Pa. YMCA	U.S. Air Force Hickman Air Force Base, Hawaii	Los Alamitos Naval Air Station, Los Alamitos, Cal.
8.	1959	Des Moines, Iowa YMCA (No. Side H.S.)	Los Alamitos Naval Air Station, Los Alamitos, Cal.	Hickman Air Force Base, Honolulu, Hawaii
9.	1960	Dallas, Texas YMCA at S. M. U.	6th Region U.S. Army Air Defense Command, Presidio, Cal.	Hamilton Air Force Base, Hamilton, Cal.
10.	1961	Duluth, Minn. YMCA, U. M. D.	6th Region U.S. Army Air Defense Command, Presidio, Cal.	Whitman AFB, Grandview, Mo.
11.	1962	Phila. Palestra	Alameda NAS	Otis AFB Buzzard Bay County, Mass.
12.	1963	San Antonio, Texas	Alameda NAS	Memphis NAS

This tournament terminated with the 1963 National Championships held in San Antonio, Texas.

WINNERS OF NATIONAL (USVBA) COLLEGIATE
VOLLEYBALL CHAMPIONSHIPS (MEN)

No.	Year	Place	Winner	Runner-up
1.	1949	Los Angeles, Cal. Downtown YMCA	Univ. of Southern California	Stanford Univ.
2.	1950	Knoxville, Tenn. YMCA	Univ. of Southern California	Univ. of Mexico
3.	1951	Springfield College, Springfield, Mass.	Univ. of Mexico, D.F.	Springfield College, Mass.
4.	1952	Columbus, Ohio Ohio State Univ.	Univ. of Mexico, D.F.	George Williams College, Chicago

No.	Year	Place	Winner	Runner-up
5.	1953	Omaha, Nebraska YMCA and Boys Town	Univ. of California at Los Angeles	Earlham College Richmond, Ind.
6.	1954	Tucson, Arizona YMCA and High School	Univ. of California at Los Angeles	Univ. of Southern California
7.	1955	Oklahoma City, Okla. YMCA	Florida State Univ. Tallahassee	College of Med. Evang., Los Angeles
8.	1956	Seattle, Wash. YMCA	Univ. of California at Los Angeles	Stanford Univ. Palo Alto, Cal.
9.	1957	Memphis, Tenn. YMCA at Millington Naval Air Station	Florida State Univ. Tallahassee	George Williams College, Chicago
10.	1958	Scranton, Pa. YMCA	Florida State Univ. Tallahassee	Univ. of Kansas, Lawrence
11.	1959	Des Moines, Iowa YMCA	George Williams College, Chicago	Univ. of Kansas, Lawrence
12.	1960	Dallas, Texas YMCA at S. M. U.	George Williams College, Chicago	Polytechnic Institute, Mexico City, Mexico
13.	1961	Duluth, Minn. YMCA at U. M. D.	City College Santa Monica, Cal.	George Williams College
14.	1962	Phila. Palestra	City College Santa Monica, Cal.	George Williams College
15.	1963	San Antonio, Texas	City College Santa Monica, Cal.	Univ. of Cal., Los Angeles
16.	1964	Air Force Academy Colorado Springs, Colo.	City College Santa Monica, Cal.	Univ. of Cal. at Los Angeles
17.	1965	Omaha, Neb. Offutt Air Force Base	Univ. of Cal. at Los Angeles	City College Santa Monica, Cal.
18.	1966	Grand Rapids, Mich. YMCA at Calvin College	City College Santa Monica, Cal.	Univ. of Cal. at Los Angeles
19.	1967	Detroit, Mich. Met. YMCA at Wayne State Univ.	Univ. of Cal. at Los Angeles	City College Santa Monica, Cal.
20.	1968	Portland, Oregon YMCA at Portland State College	San Diego State College	Church College of Hawaii

WINNERS OF NATIONAL YMCA OPEN SENIOR (FORMERLY CALLED VETERAN'S, THEN MASTER'S) VOLLEYBALL CHAMPIONSHIPS

No.	Year	Place	Winner	Runner-up
1.	1928	Chattanooga, Tenn. YMCA	Chattanooga, Tenn., YMCA	Atlanta, Ga., YMCA
2.	1929	Chicago, Ill. Hyde Park YMCA	Springfield, Ohio, YMCA	Chicago, Ill., Hyde Park YMCA
3.	1930	Columbus, Ohio Central YMCA	Lansing, Mich., YMCA	Springfield, Mo., YMCA
4.	1931	Rochester, N.Y. Central YMCA	Lansing, Mich., YMCA	Rochester, N.Y., YMCA

No.	Year	Place	Winner	Runner-up
	1932	No Veterans' Tournament		
	1933	No Veterans' Tournament		
5.	1934	Knoxville, Tenn. YMCA	Fort Wayne, Ind., YMCA	Knoxville, Tenn., YMCA
6.	1935	Binghamton, N.Y. YMCA	Fort Wayne, Ind., YMCA	Buffalo, N.Y., YMCA
7.	1936	Davenport, Iowa YMCA	Fort Wayne, Ind., YMCA	Binghamton, N.Y., YMCA
8.	1937	Louisville, Ky. YMCA	Fort Wayne, Ind., YMCA	Indianapolis, Ind., YMCA
9.	1938	Detroit, Mich. YMCA	Fort Wayne, Ind., YMCA	Indianapolis, Ind., YMCA
10.	1939	San Francisco, Cal. Embarcadero YMCA	Pasadena, Cal., YMCA	Seattle, Wash., YMCA
11.	1940	Philadelphia, Pa. Central YMCA	Fort Wayne, Ind., YMCA	Somerville, Mass., YMCA
12.	1941	Ann Arbor, Mich. YMCA at Intramural Sports Bldg.	Davenport, Iowa, YMCA	Somerville, Mass., YMCA
13.	1942	St. Paul, Minn. YMCA	Ann Arbor, Mich., YMCA	St. Paul, Minn., YMCA
14.	1946	Chicago, Ill. Hyde Park YMCA and Univ. of Chicago	Houston, Texas, YMCA	Ann Arbor, Mich., YMCA
15.	1947	Houston, Texas YMCA and at Coliseum	Greensburg, Ind., YMCA	Houston, Texas, YMCA
16.	1948	South Bend, Ind., at YMCA and John Adams High School	Minneapolis, Minn., Central YMCA	Jamaica, L.I., N.Y., YMCA
17.	1949	Los Angeles, Cal. Downtown & Hollywood Reserve Armory	San Francisco, Cal., Embarcadero YMCA	Hollywood, Cal., YMCA
18.	1950	Knoxville, Tenn. YMCA, Chilhowee Pk.	Ann Arbor, Mich., YMCA	Cincinnati, Ohio, Central YMCA
19.	1951	Springfield, College, Springfield, Mass.	Jamaica, N.Y., YMCA	Cincinnati, Ohio, Central YMCA
20.	1952	Columbus, Ohio Ohio State Univ.	Jamaica, N.Y., YMCA	Cincinnati, Ohio, Central YMCA
21.	1953	Omaha, Neb. YMCA	Omaha, Neb., YMCA	Long Beach, Cal., YMCA
22.	1954	Tucson, Ariz. YMCA	Long Beach, Cal., Central YMCA	Omaha, Neb., Central YMCA
23.	1955	Oklahoma City, Okla. YMCA	Houston, Texas, Central YMCA	New York, N.Y., West Side Br. YMCA
24.	1956	Seattle, Wash. YMCA	San Francisco, Cal., Embarcadero YMCA	Long Beach, Cal., Central YMCA
25.	1957	Memphis, Tenn. YMCA at Millington Naval Air Station	Hollywood, Cal., YMCA Comets	Detroit, Mich., Downtown YMCA

No.	Year	Place	Winner	Runner-up
26.	1958	Scranton, Pa. YMCA	Hollywood, Cal., YMCA Comets	Detroit, Mich., Downtown Br. YMCA
27.	1959	Des Moines, Iowa YMCA	Hollywood, Cal., YMCA Comets	Des Moines, Iowa YMCA
28.	1960	Dallas, Texas At S. M. U.	Hollywood, Cal., YMCA Comets	Houston, Texas, YMCA
29.	1961	Duluth, Minn. YMCA, at U. M. D.	Beverly Hills, Cal., YMCA	Minneapolis, Minn., Downtown YMCA
30.	1962	Phila. Palestra	Beverly Hills YMCA	Norristown, Pa., YMCA
31.	1963	San Antonio, Texas	Houston YMCA	L.A. West Side Jewish Community Center
32.	1964	New York City Met. YMCA at Queens College	Woonsocket, R.I. YMCA	Dallas, Texas Athletic Club
33.	1965	Omaha, Neb. Offutt Air Force Base	Los Angeles, Cal. West Side JCC	Woonsocket, R.I. YMCA
34.	1966	Grand Rapids, Mch. YMCA at Calvin College	Long Beach, Cal. Sand & Sea Club	Los Angeles, Cal. West Side JCC
35.	1967	Detroit, Mich. Met. YMCA at Wayne State Univ.	Los Angeles, Cal. West Side JCC	St. Louis, Mo. Downtown YMCA
36.	1968	Portland, Oregon YMCA at Portland State Col.	Long Beach, Cal. YMCA	Honolulu, Hawaii Outrigger Canoe Club—Green

WINNERS OF NATIONAL OPEN VOLLEYBALL CHAMPIONSHIPS (USVBA)

No.	Year	Place	Winner	Runner-up
1.	1928	Chattanooga, Tenn. YMCA	Germantown, Pa., YMCA	Chicago, Ill., Hyde Park YMCA
2.	1929	Chicago, Ill. Hyde Park YMCA	Chicago, Ill., Hyde Park YMCA	Chicago, Ill., Division St. YMCA
3.	1930	Columbus, Ohio Central YMCA	Chicago, Ill., Hyde Park YMCA	Denver, Colo., YMCA
4.	1931	Rochester, N.Y. Central YMCA	San Antonio, Texas, YMCA	Chicago, Ill., Division St. YMCA
5.	1932	Chicago, Ill. Hyde Park YMCA	San Antonio, Texas, YMCA	Chicago, Ill., Hyde Park YMCA
6.	1933	Chicago, Ill., By YMCA at Naval Reserve Armory	Houston, Texas, YMCA	Chicago, Ill., Hyde Park YMCA
7.	1934	Knoxville, Tenn. YMCA	Houston, Texas, YMCA	Chicago, Ill., Division St. YMCA
8.	1935	Binghamton, N.Y. YMCA	Houston, Texas, YMCA	Chicago, Ill., Division St. YMCA
9.	1936	Davenport, Iowa YMCA	Houston, Texas, YMCA	Philadelphia, Pa., North Br. YMCA
10.	1937	Louisville, Ky. YMCA	Chicago, Ill., Duncan, YMCA	Philadelphia, Pa., North Br. YMCA

No.	Year	Place	Winner	Runner-up
11.	1938	Detroit, Mich. Downtown YMCA	Houston, Texas, YMCA	Davenport, Iowa YMCA
12.	1939	San Francisco, Cal. Embarcadero YMCA	Houston, Texas, YMCA	Los Angeles, Cal., Los Angeles Athletic Club
13.	1940	Phila., Central YMCA At Penn Athletic Club	Los Angeles, Cal., L.A. Athletic Club	Houston, Texas, YMCA
14.	1941	Ann Arbor, Mich. YMCA	Chicago, Ill., North Ave. Larrabee YMCA	Houston, Texas, YMCA
15.	1942	St. Paul, Minn. YMCA	Chicago, Ill., North Ave. Larrabee YMCA	Philadelphia, Pa., Central YMCA
16.	1945	Minneapolis, Minn. Central YMCA	Chicago, Ill., North Ave. Larrabee YMCA	Jamaica, L.I., N.Y., YMCA
17.	1946	Chicago, Ill. Hyde Park YMCA	Pasadena, Cal., YMCA	Los Angeles, Cal., Los Angeles Athletic Club
18.	1947	Houston, Texas YMCA	Chicago, Ill., North Ave. Larrabee YMCA	Pasadena, Cal., YMCA
19.	1948	South Bend, Ind. YMCA and John Adams High School	Hollywood, Cal., YMCA	Los Angeles, Cal., Downtown YMCA
20.	1949	Los Angeles, Cal. Downtown & Holly-wood YMCA, at Naval Reserve Armory	Los Angeles, Cal., Downtown YMCA	Long Beach, Cal., YMCA
21.	1950	Knoxville, Tenn. YMCA	Long Beach, Cal., YMCA	Hollywood, Cal., YMCA
22.	1951	Springfield, Mass. Springfield College	Hollywood, Cal., YMCA	Chicago, Ill., North Ave. YMCA
23.	1952	Columbus, Ohio Ohio State Univ.	Hollywood, Cal., YMCA	Stockton, Cal., YMCA
24.	1953	Omaha, Neb. YMCA	Hollywood, Cal., YMCA	Long Beach, Cal., YMCA
25.	1954	Tucson, Ariz. YMCA and H.S.	Stockton, Cal., YMCA	Hollywood, Cal., YMCA Stars
26.	1955	Oklahoma City, Okla. YMCA	Stockton, Cal., YMCA	Hollywood, Cal., YMCA Stars
27.	1956	Seattle, Wash. YMCA	Hollywood, Cal., YMCA Stars	Stockton, Cal., YMCA
28.	1957	Memphis, Tenn. YMCA at Millington Naval Air Station	Hollywood, Cal., YMCA Stars	Stockton, Cal., YMCA
29.	1958	Scranton, Pa. YMCA	Hollywood, Cal., YMCA Stars	Los Angeles, Cal., Westside Jewish Community Center
30.	1959	Des Moines, Iowa YMCA (No. Side H.S.)	Hollywood, Cal., YMCA Stars	Los Angeles, Cal., Westside Jewish Community Center

No.	Year	Place	Winner	Runner-up
31.	1960	Dallas, Texas YMCA (at S. M. U.)	Los Angeles, Cal., Westside Jewish Community Center	Hollywood, Cal., YMCA Stars
32.	1961	Duluth, Minn. YMCA at U. M .D.	Hollywood, Cal., YMCA	Los Angeles, Cal., Westside Jewish Community Center
33.	1962	Phila. Palestra	Hollywood YMCA	Pasadena YMCA
34.	1963	Ft. Sam Houston San Antonio, Texas	Hollywood YMCA	Stockton YMCA
35.	1964	New York City Met. YMCA at Queens College	Hollywood, Cal., YMCA Stars	Long Beach, Cal. Century Club
36.	1965	Omaha, Neb. Offutt Air Force Base	Los Angeles, Cal. Westside JCC	Los Angeles, Cal. Tigers
37.	1966	Grand Rapids, Mich. YMCA at Calvin College	Long Beach, Cal. Sand & Sea Club	Honolulu, Hawaii Outrigger Club
38.	1967	Detroit, Mich. Met. YMCA at Wayne State Univ.	Fresno, Cal. V.C.	Cal. Sand & Sea Tigers
39.	1968	Portland, Oregon YMCA at Portland State Col.	Los Angeles, Cal. Westside JCC	Honolulu, Hawaii Outrigger Canoe Club—White

PAN AMERICAN GAMES VOLLEYBALL CHAMPIONSHIP

(Men's Division)

No.	Year	Place	Winner	Runner-up
1.	1955	Mexico City	U.S.A.	Mexico
2.	1959	Chicago, Ill.	U.S.A.	Brazil
3.	1963	Sao Paulo, Brazil	Brazil	U.S.A.

(Women's Division)

No.	Year	Place	Winner	Runner-up
1.	1955	Mexico City	Mexico	U.S.A.
2.	1959	Chicago, Ill.	Brazil	U.S.A.
3.	1963	Sao Paulo, Brazil	Brazil	U.S.A.

WORLD VOLLEYBALL CHAMPIONSHIPS
CONDUCTED BY INTERNATIONAL VOLLEYBALL FEDERATION

(Men's Division)

	No.	Year	Place	Winner	Runner-up
(10 teams)	1	1949	Prague	U.S.S.R.	Czechoslovakia
(11 teams)	2	1952	Moscow	U.S.S.R.	Czechoslovakia
(24 teams)	3	1956	Paris	Czechoslovakia (U.S.A. 6th)	Roumania
(12 teams)	4	1960	Brazil	U.S.S.R. (U.S.A. 6th)	Czechoslovakia
(10 teams)	5	1962	Moscow	U.S.S.R.	Czechoslovakia

(Women's Division)		Place		Winner	Runner-up
(8 teams)	1	1952	Moscow	U.S.S.R.	Poland
(17 teams)	2	1956	Paris	U.S.S.R. (U.S.A. 9th)	Roumania
(10 teams)	3	1960	Brazil	U.S.S.R. (U.S.A. 6th)	Japan
(8 teams)	4	1962	Moscow	Japan	U.S.S.R.

OYMPIC GAMES

(Men's Division)	Place		Winner	Runner-up	
1.	1964	Tokyo, Japan	U.S.S.R.	Czechoslovakia	(USA 9th)
2.	1968	Mexico City, Mexico	U.S.S.R.	Japan	(USA 7th)
3.	1972	Munich, Germany	Japan	East Germany	
			(USA did not make the Munich finals)		

(Women's Division)	Place		Winner	Runner-up	
1.	1964	Tokyo, Japan	Japan	U.S.S.R.	(USA 5th)
2.	1968	Mexico City, Mexico	U.S.S.R.	Japan	(USA 8th)
3.	1972	Munich, Germany	U.S.S.R.	Japan	
			(USA did not make the Munich finals)		

index

4302-4-
5-14
C